# CANCER

## 21 June - 22 July

## *Your horoscope for 2020*

The complete 12-month forecast

ROCKPOOL
PUBLISHING

♋

Patsy Bennett is a rare combination of astrologer and psychic medium. Her horoscopes are published in over 65 newspapers and magazines throughout Australia and internationally. She is a speaker, provides astrology and psychic consultations and holds astrology and psychic development workshops in Byron Bay, Australia, where she lives.

Patsy runs www.astrocast.com.au, www.patsybennett.com, facebook @patsybennettpsychicastrology and insta@patsybennettastrology.

A Rockpool book
PO Box 252
Summer Hill, NSW 2130
www.rockpoolpublishing.com.au
www.facebook.com/rockpoolpublishing

First published in 2019


ISBN 978-1-925924-03-9

Design by Tracy Loughlin, Rockpool Publishing
Editing by Lisa Macken
Illustrations by Shutterstock
Printed and bound in China

10 9 8 7 6 5 4 3 2 1

# Contents

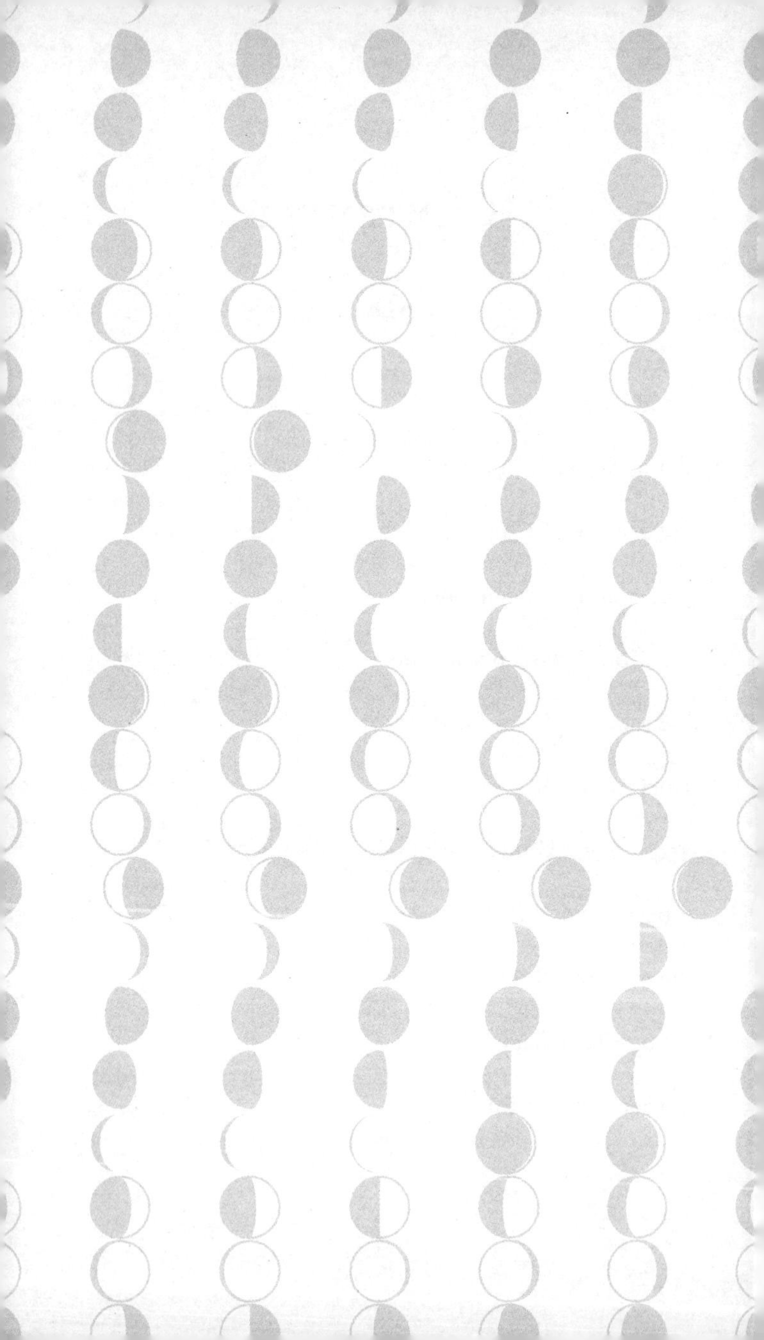

# Introduction

Make 2020 your best year yet! Start the year with 20/20 vision: clearly see your amazing year ahead for love, luck, loot and lifestyle. We all consult our horoscopes, but what we really want to know is how best to plan ahead for ourselves personally. Astrology is the study of the movement of celestial objects and their impact on us here on earth, but we need to know what that means on an individual level.

The key throughout the year is to be proactive. This guide doesn't just show you when good things will happen to you. It also shows you how to view positive astrological days as opportunities to initiate new ideas, organise wonderful events and let love into your life, and to see challenging days as days to excel, to draw on your inner reserves and find success by overcoming obstacles. Your greatest achievements will often occur when you conquer hurdles and allow your inner hero to rise to the challenge.

In *Your Horoscope for 2020: Cancer* you'll find insight into your own strengths and weaknesses, and into your own way to move ahead month by month in astrological circumstances. Find out top times for travel, love, communications, domestic circumstances and health and wealth development according to *your* sun sign. With the benefit of a little foresight, this information will go a long way to making 2020 an extremely rewarding year.

Success is all in the timing and in knowing what to do with your own strengths in mind, and there's no better time than the present to consult your own guide to success in 2020. This really is the year you can embrace your own star power: starting now!

## Glyphs for each sun sign

| Constellation | Symbol/Glyph | Ruling planet | Element |
|---|---|---|---|
| Aries | Ram ♈ | Mars | Fire |
| Taurus | Bull ♉ | Venus | Earth |
| Gemini | Twins ♊ | Mercury | Air |
| Cancer | Crab ♋ | Moon | Water |
| Leo | Lion ♌ | Sun | Fire |
| Virgo | Virgin ♍ | Mercury | Earth |
| Libra | Scales ♎ | Venus | Air |
| Scorpio | Scorpion ♏ | Mars, Pluto | Water |
| Sagittarius | Archer ♐ | Jupiter | Fire |
| Capricorn | Goat ♑ | Saturn | Earth |
| Aquarius | Water bearer ♒ | Uranus, Saturn | Air |
| Pisces | Fish ♓ | Jupiter, Neptune | Water |

# The essence of Cancer

One of the three water signs, you are a caring and intuitive character; you are also one of the strongest members of the zodiac family. A cardinal sign, you have a backbone beyond your own understanding and often only discover your strength when you are challenged and in the midst of difficult circumstances. You're generally known for your sensitive side and yet you can be a live wire when you're motivated.

You're better known to circumnavigate trouble and then duck into your shell when under attack, which is why a crab is the symbol for your sign: you tend to walk sideways! Even so, try as you may to circumnavigate trouble you will nevertheless encounter various challenges that will demand you step up and be the strong character you are regardless of the sensitivity that lies beneath the tough shell you hide under. You really are tough through and through, so don't buy into the idea that you're not!

Family, caring for others and being part of a strong social fabric are all very important to you. Nurturance, both in the form of a good diet and emotional support, is also critical, and this is an area in your life you are likely to embrace wholeheartedly. When you think your genuine caring feelings for someone are not being reciprocated you can feel let down, ultimately withdrawing your affections as a result. It is only after a long, hard, extended period of caregiving and nurturance that you give freely.

You may be relatively slower than many other signs to commit to someone, but when you do your feelings run deep and you'll find it hard to extricate yourself from a relationship. Always consult your very accurate instincts when you're choosing friends and a partner.

## Self-esteem

One of your true inner resources is that you have high self-esteem and are not afraid to leave your comfort zone to attain your goals. You are adventurous in your interpersonal dealings, especially financially and emotionally. Even if you are shy as a youngster, you know you have inner mettle and determination. You are open to new projects and ideas that other less courageous characters might avoid.

You may wish for a wonderful romantic and marriage partner, not only because of your fondness for home life and family but also because you enjoy the stability and security that a partnership can bring. Once committed to a relationship you will not want to relinquish it, but make no mistake: if you feel that your trust is being abused it will take a long time to reinstate it. If respect and equality don't reign in your relationship you have the strength to quickly annul the partnership.

In business you are a solid partner but may be reluctant to move forward with innovations and fresh ideas, so always be ready to look for ways to move ahead in your business and personal collaborations.

You are an imaginative and creative character and fiction, story-writing, singing, music and theatre will all appeal to your appreciation of artistic areas. Little Cancerians should be encouraged to express themselves through art at a young age.

Sport will also appeal to the active Cancerian, as it is a great way to teach youngsters how to channel their strong energy into action and activities.

## Your inner life

Beneath the hard exterior we know there's a soft crab inside, yet what is less known about you is that the sensitivity that characterises you is more to do with your psychic and intuitive abilities and instincts and less to do with your shyness and fear. This isn't to say you're not a shy character – when young you can certainly appear this way – but you're a natural-born sensitive who can feel undercurrents that other zodiac signs may not be aware of. You're able to understand the undercurrents of circumstances and may feel these more readily than other more earthy signs.

Being a sensitive character you can tend to take other people's problems as your own, a true pitfall of the empath. You'll shoulder other people's problems and want to help them and offer support, so much so that sometimes you will mistakenly see their issues as being your issues. The problem is that you are then less able to help because you are ensconced in the problem rather than being an agent for solution. Other people must sort out their own problems, irrespective of your help.

Once you mature and are more assertive and can see the fine line between your life and other people's lives you will

be a more effective nurturer and carer, and will also have an understanding of your own responsibility to self first and foremost and then to others.

## How to maximise your potential

Finding your voice is the most important aspect of your self-development, which you can go about in many ways. Public speaking is a good conduit to self-expression and assertiveness. You'll appreciate the opportunity of getting up in front of a crowd of strangers, becoming more open and overcoming feelings of shyness or self-doubt. Finding a toastmaster's club that teaches you how to speak clearly will be a wonderful way to move forward with your self-expression.

Storytelling, writing and talking are all activities that will soothe your soul. You won't necessarily be a bestselling author, a speaker on the international circuit or the person weaving mystery and magic at writer's festivals – although there's nothing to say you can't be – but all these creative past-times will bring your inner creativity out and help you to connect with friends and family.

To be the best you can be, become conscious that you do, in fact, have strong intuition and even psychic powers. Enrolling in a psychic development class won't necessarily mean you will become a professional psychic, but you will learn the many tips and techniques necessary to use this most important faculty.

Being so naturally inclined to homemaking, family and nesting, you'll find that the more stable and secure you feel at home and domestically the more stable and secure you will feel in yourself.

In your profession, homemaking, property, maintenance or hospitality will appeal because the place where people rest is the one that attracts you the most.

Because you tend to be easily influenced it's important to establish a strong sense of self and a strong set of ethical codes and values, otherwise you will tend to be drawn this way and that by life's many distractions, activities and personalities. When you realise that you are being led by others or feel you are not expressing your highest sense of purpose, it's important to re-align your activities with your heart-centred code of values and ethics.

## How others see you

Cancer is ruled by the moon, so you can tend to be seen as being moody. The moon changes signs every two days and you can, as a result, be someone who changes their mind and whose feelings fluctuate fairly frequently. You may be accused of being up and down, and while this may be true you can find out how to work with lunar energy so you are less flighty and more stable.

If you know your moon sign at birth (the sign the moon was in when you were born you will know that when the moon is in this sign you will be at your most rock steady and potent, barring any afflictions to the moon in your astrological chart). Keep an eye on how you feel during the various phases of the moon; self-knowledge is one of the best tools to contentedness.

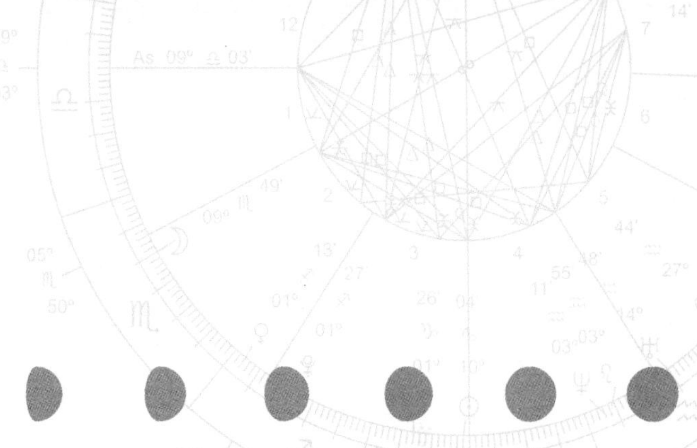

# Cancer and its ascendants

This book is about your sun sign, Cancer, and your predictions for the year ahead. The more you know about yourself the better you will be able to take advantage of opportunities, and also to avoid the pitfalls. It's critical to know as much about 'you' as possible.

In astrology your core self is represented by your sun sign, but did you know that your personality traits are represented by your ascendant (also known as your rising sign)?The ascendant describes your personality, the way other people see you on first meeting you and the way you tend to filter life's events.

When you have intimate knowledge about your sun sign – your engine room or core being – you will be on the way to a happier life. When you add the knowledge about your personality – your ascendant – you will gain even deeper insight into what makes you tick.

Your ascendant sign is determined by the time of your birth on the date and year of your birth. Because your ascendant sign changes approximately every two hours, the best way to determine it is to ask an astrologer to calculate it for you.

Certain apps will also calculate your ascendant sign (see page 155).

The following gives you more information about your abilities, characteristics and personality according to your sun sign Cancer in combination with your ascendant sign.

## Cancer sun sign with Aries ascendant

You are a force to be reckoned with: two cardinal signs in such prominent positions points to a strong character. You can be stubborn, especially if your will is opposed, but you are also a gentle, introspective person underneath, which may be quite surprising to those who get to know you better.

The Aries personality can project a reckless, at times bossy, fiery or even domineering exterior, yet your Cancerian sensitivity lies quietly beneath this strong outer avatar. You have extrasensory perception, as the Cancerian core enables you to intuit information about people and circumstances despite your fiery or brash Aries. Despite your sensitivity you have inner resourcefulness that indicates great strength of character.

## Cancer sun sign with Taurus ascendant

The combination of an earth sign and a water sign provides you with abilities that span the divide between the rational and the intuitive, giving you superpowers! The Taurean ascendant enables you to be steadfast, practical and grounded, while the Cancerian core enables you to garner information about people and circumstances that other sun signs don't perceive. Combine the steadiness of the Taurus personality and the instincts of the inner Cancerian, and you really are a force to be reckoned with. The Taurean personality is diligent and strong, and once your mind is made up there is little that can change it; your main pitfall is obstinacy. Aim to be more adaptable, and you'll find your options widen immeasurably.

## Cancer sun sign with Gemini ascendant

You are a seemingly happy-go-lucky character, but underneath your bravado lies an inner warmth and gentleness; this is your Cancerian core. On the surface your Gemini personality is able to detach from emotional circumstances that irk you while you appear to remain carefree. Any pain you feel is then on a deeper level and can manifest as moodiness, which can be confusing to those who see you as being light-hearted and fun loving and may even surprise you. As you mature you will feel more in tune with yourself and able to merge both intellect and emotions into a balanced, well-rounded character.

## Cancer sun sign with Cancer ascendant

You are a double Cancer and, as such, are doubly intuitive and strong and a leader. But you are also doubly moody, introverted and cantankerous when the mood takes you! The key to making this combination work for you is to maximise your best qualities and minimise your worst. Make your intuitive abilities work for you; see them as an inner radar that guides you to making the right decisions, and your life will become so much easier. Don't let sensitivity deter you from your core strength; you are a leader and you feel fulfilled when you take action. Manage moodiness and find ways to avoid sinking into an introverted cycle, by joining groups and being outgoing and sociable. You can be easily distracted and may be prone to

overindulge in the good things in life, so keep an eye on these tendencies.

## Cancer sun sign with Leo ascendant

You have a dynamo personality that can appear to be brash at times. Your fiery Leo get up and go personality works well with the iron will of your Cancerian inner self, but when you impulsively charge ahead your sensitive, caring Cancer may take some time to catch up with your own impulsiveness! This can lead to inner tension or disappointment.

Once you learn when to take action and when to allow your intuition to lead a little more the Cancer sun sign with the Leo ascendant makes a strong character able to stand your own ground and lead the pack. Combined with your sixth sense, this is a self-motivated combination and is quite a force to be reckoned with.

## Cancer sun sign with Virgo ascendant

This combination can be effective, as your practical personality will enable the sensitive, intuitive Cancerian core to take action in methodical and measured ways. The care and attention you take in life is admirable, but you must make sure your ideals and values are effective as your practical personality will enable the sensitive, intuitive Cancerian core to take action. You are a caring personality who wishes the world to be one big contented, healthy and positive family, so you can become disheartened when faced with the reality that humans are not perfect. You will work towards improving the health and well-being of others in admirable ways. Self-care must always come first, or you will burn out due to the near impossible tasks you tend to set yourself.

## Cancer sun sign with Libra ascendant

Two cardinal signs in such prominent positions points to a strong personality. Your strength of character may come as a surprise even to you, as you are generally known to have a soft, gentle approach to life. You love music, art, reading, writing and romance but you can be stubborn, especially if your will is opposed. If you feel your will is being challenged it will be hard to change your mind. You do have extrasensory perception, as your Cancerian core can intuit information about people and circumstances that other signs don't perceive. Combine this with your search for peace and harmony in life and you really are a gentle and perceptive yet strong and determined character.

## Cancer sun sign with Scorpio ascendant

You are a double water sign and are intuitive, emotional and sometimes super moody. Being moody is no surprise, as you feel your way through life and are a truly empathic character; your moods swing in line with the atmosphere, room or event you are experiencing. As a youngster these qualities may be confusing, as there is little in common between your intuitive approach and the reasoning world. As a youngster you may be easily misled and influenced. You have artistic, even psychic abilities and tend to overindulge in the good things in life, so must avoid co-dependent and addictive behaviour. You will find balance in life by seeing the world through both your practical eyes and your intuitive, artistic senses.

## Cancer sun sign with Sagittarius ascendant

You are quite the dynamo: upbeat, outgoing, adventurous and a daredevil. The outgoing Sagittarian personality will often mask the gentler yet resolute Cancerian underneath. It will take some time for people to meet the sensitive Cancerian, as the gregarious Sagittarian qualities will take the lead. The care and attention you take in life is admirable, and you are also an upbeat character. There will be an interest in writing, study and storytelling. You may be a chatterbox, especially once you feel comfortable in your surroundings, but you may also be protective of your inner qualities such as your sixth sense. Take your time to cultivate your inner self; your intuition is an additional string to your bow.

## Cancer sun sign with Capricorn ascendant

Two cardinal signs in prominent positions can lead to stubbornness, especially when you are opposed. Yet your Capricorn personality, the self people see on first meeting you, appears to be down to earth, reasonable and quiet. The Cancerian inner self can also make you appear to be a gentle, introspective person, but when you are challenged your inner resourcefulness and ability to stand your ground will be quite surprising.

You may feel an inner tension between being gentle and perceptive on the one hand and being practical and down to earth on the other. If so, take the time to work on combining your gentleness and earthiness and you will become truly rounded. Combine your Cancerian instincts with the steadfastness of the Capricorn character, and you should find your path an easier one.

## Cancer sun sign with Aquarius ascendant

You are quite the personality: quirky, independent, outgoing, even eccentric and upbeat one day then quiet, traditional and retiring the next. You may be seen as being unusual or as a chameleon. Others with less adaptability will marvel at your ability to mix in with any circumstance, and your adaptability, flexibility and open-mindedness are certainly useful qualities. You are also resolute and determined and can be super stubborn. Depending on the day, you display some or all of these traits! A true pitfall would be to manifest only the negative traits, which include your occasional inability to see the opinions of others and your closed-mindedness and obstinacy. Luckily, your eccentricity means you are rarely stuck in any one particular mindset, which is both a blessing and potentially a difficulty. Mindfulness and meditation work supremely well for you to make you more centred.

## Cancer sun sign with Pisces ascendant

You are an emotional and intuitive character; two water signs in such prominent positions point to a sensitive character who has deeper perception than many other people. Your Cancerian core self is a gentle, introspective person who is also resourceful and able to stand your ground. This ability may be quite a surprise for those who see only the gentle and dreamy Pisces personality on first meeting. However, the Pisces willpower is also rock solid, with outward gentleness belying inner strength.

You do have a certain extrasensory perception, as both the Cancerian traits and the Piscean psychic abilities make for a supremely intuitive individual. This sensitivity can sometimes lead you to being easily misled and fooled, so base important decisions on facts, not influence.

# THE MOON'S PART IN YOUR LIFE

Your sun sign is Cancer, which represents your core self. Your ascendant informs you about your personality and how other people see you on first meeting, while your moon sign informs you about your emotional make-up. The moon changes signs every two days so, depending on where you were born and at what time, your moon sign will be different. To find out your moon sign it's best to consult an astrologer to guarantee you receive accurate information (see also page 155). There are also signs for the placements of all the planets at the time of your birth, and astrologers will consider all of this information when providing a personal consultation for you.

You will find you begin to gain considerable insight into who you are when you combine the information about your moon sign with information about your sun sign and ascendant. It will enable you to choose your best qualities and consciously promote these and minimise your worse qualities, helping you to be the best person you can be.

You will find that when the moon is in your sign, as listed day by day in the calendar, life is either easier or more

challenging depending on the planetary aspects to your moon at the time of your birth. Keep a note of the general mood and occurrences when the moon is in your sign as it will enable you to plan ahead more readily with the full knowledge that you can do so according to the sun, moon and stars.

The following pages in this section give a detailed description of your moon sign.

## Moon in Aries

You tend to be outgoing in your emotional life and will enter relationships on impulse. Your ardour may fire up as rapidly as it wanes, and you can lose interest quickly if you feel your affections are not reciprocated. Always consider carefully who you wish to give your emotional energy and time to, as you may otherwise blow hot and cold. You tend to have a hot temper. Having both the sun and the moon in Aries is a double fire sign, and means you can lose interest quickly in your projects. Take the time to formulate plans and stick to them, or you will tend to lose enthusiasm and leave many projects unfinished. You have a child-like enthusiasm that is endearing; when you mature your fervour for life could give you an enduringly youthful and fun-loving demeanour.

## Moon in Taurus

A Taurean moon can provide a sensual, calm emotional state, and when you're involved with a Taurean moon person you're likely to enjoy romantic events such as candlelit dinners, good cooking, good-quality clothes and furnishings and open fireplaces where you warm your toes on a cold winter's night.

A Taurean moon person is someone who values friendship and mutual support and has an appreciation for all things luxurious. Some Taurean moon people can be self-centred, due to your high self-esteem. Another pitfall is a predilection to over-indulgence in all the finer things in life and an unwillingness to see the other side of the coin.

## Moon in Gemini

Moon in Gemini people tend to be talkative and are likely to reach out to others, although they also like to retain a sense of independence and, when under pressure, will even appear to be detached emotionally. You intellectualise and compartmentalise your emotions, seeming to switch them on and off, which may be infuriating to those who depend on you for support. This may make you appear to be two-faced, yet you are simply embracing the many various qualities you have. You will often find in life you need to agree to disagree with people who cannot see differing points of view.

A Gemini moon person gives emotional support but not in ways you might expect due to your sense of independence and detachment. You get on well with the other air signs, Libra and Aquarius, and with anyone who has the ability to be emotionally independent while still being a loving and supportive character.

## Moon in Cancer

Yours is a fundamentally sensitive emotional make-up. You can be driven by strong emotions, which can take over your thoughts, so it's important to find ways to establish balance in your mind. If you allow emotional expression to overwhelm

your intellect and intuition you can feel out of sorts and make mistakes.

You are a hugely intuitive person and may have innate psychic abilities. You need to differentiate between intuition, psychic impressions and emotionally driven impulses so you can be guided by your inner compass rather than being overwhelmed by emotions. Home and family will be important to you, and you are loyal to those you love.

## Moon in Leo

You like to initiate fun projects and are an active, outgoing, emotionally demonstrative and playful character. Being playful may make you seem insincere in your emotional entanglements. You sometimes enter relationships on a whim, only to discover you have no interest or affection for the person you have befriended.

You are unlikely to be a wallflower at social events unless you have planets in sensitive signs in your natal chart. Emotionally you are bold and outgoing and like to be the centre of attention. You're a loyal family member who takes your close interpersonal relationships very seriously. At home you will be the queen or king of the jungle.

## Moon in Virgo

You are considered and careful and unlikely to rush into relationships without forethought (unless you have a strong fire signature in your birth chart). You are unlikely to fall head over heels in love one day and disappear the next, as you like constancy in relationships and exhibit a constancy in your own emotional make-up. You are an earthy person, preferring to take your emotional life step by step. Once you make a commitment it is likely to be long-standing; you do not take responsibilities and duties lightly. In your love life you look for perfection so can tend to be critical, not only of others but also of yourself. You'll take a little time to assimilate that no one is perfect.

You may tend to be choosy about who you bring into your personal inner circle. Professionally you are dependable and hard working.

## Moon in Libra

You look for emotional balance and perfection in relationships, both in your love life and at work. Perfect harmony and peace not always possible, as you learn and hone your interpersonal skills throughout your lifetime. Throughout that process you can tend to seesaw up and down through triumphs and dissatisfactions, and success and disappointment. You can be unbalanced emotionally because of your indecision and wish for that elusive perfect X factor. Work actively towards balancing your emotions and you will succeed in gaining what you're looking for. This can be achieved through meditation, yoga and exercise, and your demeanour will attract balanced partners, friends and family.

## Moon in Scorpio

You are a passionate character who is likely to enter into tempestuous relationships that can extend to the edges of every emotion you've ever felt. While deep, intense, transformative experiences may be exciting and happy, you risk delving into destructive emotional cycles that take your every breath to reconcile. You have an enigmatic and charming emotional presence that is captivating. As you have incredible magnetism it's vital you use this carefully or you risk breaking hearts. You're the one most likely to be wounded by your own intensity, as negative emotions such as jealousy, anger and envy can overwhelm more rational thoughts. Conversely, you are a loyal person who can feel deeply committed to the people around you such as family members.

## Moon in Sagittarius

You are a bright and adventurous character who is unafraid to push yourself forwards into circumstances that others may find daring, such as living in a foreign culture or travelling for extensive periods. You are happy to try all kinds of relationships. However, as you are emotionally self-sufficient you don't actually need them. This independence means it can be difficult to develop a deep relationship with you, but because you are playful, optimistic and fun loving you will often have a large circle of friends and associates. Once you commit to someone you will give them the world.

You are a truly sincere, honest friend, family member and partner, although sometimes your honesty can sting. Moon in Sagittarius is honest to a fault: you see yourself and others through the eyes of blunt honesty rather than flattery.

## Moon in Capricorn

You can appear to be emotionally cool and calm unless your astrology chart has a strong fire element. You are practical in your endeavours and will shape your emotions rationally, leading to the appearance that you are calculating. Once you have a desired outcome in mind you certainly have the capacity to very patiently pursue your goals.

Of all the moon signs you are the one most likely to be a social climber, as you have an emotional need to succeed. You will do what it takes to do so, either by way of hard work, marriage or socialising with people you know can further your agenda.

You express your emotions by action and touch rather than through words, and as such you make an earthy, sensual lover. You have strong parental feelings towards others and will wish to guide and shape, protect and nurture those you love, even if in a seemingly cool or detached way.

## Moon in Aquarius

You have an emotional need to be different, which you may express through work, relationships or past-times that challenge the norm. You are quite the enigma, as you can be deeply committed to people or things and then very quickly change your mind and become detached. This may make you seem unreliable, quixotic or downright cruel to those who become emotionally entangled with you. Always be prepared to build bridges.

You wish to experience depth in your feelings, and when this does not seem possible you pursue new adventures in life, testing society's rules and moral codes in the process.

## Moon in Pisces

You are a truly sensitive character and may wonder why you can be moody or why your emotions fluctuate from low to high and back again for no apparent reason. Consider yourself a kind of emotional barometer: you subconsciously pick up on undercurrents that will be felt by you as emotions. For example, you may enter a room where an argument had taken place and become angry for no apparent reason. You will reflect, feel and echo someone's love for you, even if the love does not originate from you.

It's vital for you to get a good grip on your own emotions, as you can be easily influenced. Take the time to connect with your intuition, too, to ascertain the true compass in your soul that guides you through life. You have innately strong psychic abilities, which you may wish to develop.

# The moon's phases for the year

The moon's phases, including eclipses, new moons and full moons, can all affect your mood. All of these events are explained and listed in the diary, enabling you to plan ahead with the full knowledge you're moving in synchronicity with the sun and the moon.

On the following four pages are the moon's phases for 2020.

## 2020 SOUTHERN HEMISPHERE MOON PHASES

**JANUARY**

| S | M | T | W | T | F | S |
|---|---|---|---|---|---|---|
| | | | 1 | 2 | 3 | 4 |
| 5 | 6 | 7 | 8 | 9 | 10 | 11 |
| 12 | 13 | 14 | 15 | 16 | 17 | 18 |
| 19 | 20 | 21 | 22 | 23 | 24 | 25 |
| 26 | 27 | 28 | 29 | 30 | 31 | |

**FEBRUARY**

| S | M | T | W | T | F | S |
|---|---|---|---|---|---|---|
| | | | | | | 1 |
| 2 | 3 | 4 | 5 | 6 | 7 | 8 |
| 9 | 10 | 11 | 12 | 13 | 14 | 15 |
| 16 | 17 | 18 | 19 | 20 | 21 | 22 |
| 23 | 24 | 25 | 26 | 27 | 28 | 29 |

**MARCH**

| S | M | T | W | T | F | S |
|---|---|---|---|---|---|---|
| 1 | 2 | 3 | 4 | 5 | 6 | 7 |
| 8 | 9 | 10 | 11 | 12 | 13 | 14 |
| 15 | 16 | 17 | 18 | 19 | 20 | 21 |
| 22 | 23 | 24 | 25 | 26 | 27 | 28 |
| 29 | 30 | 31 | | | | |

**APRIL**

| S | M | T | W | T | F | S |
|---|---|---|---|---|---|---|
| | | | 1 | 2 | 3 | 4 |
| 5 | 6 | 7 | 8 | 9 | 10 | 11 |
| 12 | 13 | 14 | 15 | 16 | 17 | 18 |
| 19 | 20 | 21 | 22 | 23 | 24 | 25 |
| 26 | 27 | 28 | 29 | 30 | | |

**MAY**

| S | M | T | W | T | F | S |
|---|---|---|---|---|---|---|
| 31 | | | | | 1 | 2 |
| 3 | 4 | 5 | 6 | 7 | 8 | 9 |
| 10 | 11 | 12 | 13 | 14 | 15 | 16 |
| 17 | 18 | 19 | 20 | 21 | 22 | 23 |
| 24 | 25 | 26 | 27 | 28 | 29 | 30 |

**JUNE**

| S | M | T | W | T | F | S |
|---|---|---|---|---|---|---|
| | 1 | 2 | 3 | 4 | 5 | 6 |
| 7 | 8 | 9 | 10 | 11 | 12 | 13 |
| 14 | 15 | 16 | 17 | 18 | 19 | 20 |
| 21 | 22 | 23 | 24 | 25 | 26 | 27 |
| 28 | 29 | 30 | | | | |

## 2020 SOUTHERN HEMISPHERE MOON PHASES

**JULY**

| S | M | T | W | T | F | S |
|---|---|---|---|---|---|---|
| | | | 1 | 2 | 3 | 4 |
| 5 | 6 | 7 | 8 | 9 | 10 | 11 |
| 12 | 13 | 14 | 15 | 16 | 17 | 18 |
| 19 | 20 | 21 | 22 | 23 | 24 | 25 |
| 26 | 27 | 28 | 29 | 30 | 31 | |

**AUGUST**

| S | M | T | W | T | F | S |
|---|---|---|---|---|---|---|
| 30 | 31 | | | | | 1 |
| 2 | 3 | 4 | 5 | 6 | 7 | 8 |
| 9 | 10 | 11 | 12 | 13 | 14 | 15 |
| 16 | 17 | 18 | 19 | 20 | 21 | 22 |
| 23 | 24 | 25 | 26 | 27 | 28 | 29 |

**SEPTEMBER**

| S | M | T | W | T | F | S |
|---|---|---|---|---|---|---|
| | | 1 | 2 | 3 | 4 | 5 |
| 6 | 7 | 8 | 9 | 10 | 11 | 12 |
| 13 | 14 | 15 | 16 | 17 | 18 | 19 |
| 20 | 21 | 22 | 23 | 24 | 25 | 26 |
| 27 | 28 | 29 | 30 | | | |

**OCTOBER**

| S | M | T | W | T | F | S |
|---|---|---|---|---|---|---|
| | | | | 1 | 2 | 3 |
| 4 | 5 | 6 | 7 | 8 | 9 | 10 |
| 11 | 12 | 13 | 14 | 15 | 16 | 17 |
| 18 | 19 | 20 | 21 | 22 | 23 | 24 |
| 25 | 26 | 27 | 28 | 29 | 30 | 31 |

**NOVEMBER**

| S | M | T | W | T | F | S |
|---|---|---|---|---|---|---|
| 1 | 2 | 3 | 4 | 5 | 6 | 7 |
| 8 | 9 | 10 | 11 | 12 | 13 | 14 |
| 15 | 16 | 17 | 18 | 19 | 20 | 21 |
| 22 | 23 | 24 | 25 | 26 | 27 | 28 |
| 29 | 30 | | | | | |

**DECEMBER**

| S | M | T | W | T | F | S |
|---|---|---|---|---|---|---|
| | | 1 | 2 | 3 | 4 | 5 |
| 6 | 7 | 8 | 9 | 10 | 11 | 12 |
| 13 | 14 | 15 | 16 | 17 | 18 | 19 |
| 20 | 21 | 22 | 23 | 24 | 25 | 26 |
| 27 | 28 | 29 | 30 | 31 | | |

○ New moon ● Full moon

## 2020 NORTHERN HEMISPHERE MOON PHASES

### JANUARY

| S | M | T | W | T | F | S |
|---|---|---|---|---|---|---|
| | | | 1 | 2 | 3 | 4 |
| 5 | 6 | 7 | 8 | 9 | 10 | 11 |
| 12 | 13 | 14 | 15 | 16 | 17 | 18 |
| 19 | 20 | 21 | 22 | 23 | 24 | 25 |
| 26 | 27 | 28 | 29 | 30 | 31 | |

### FEBRUARY

| S | M | T | W | T | F | S |
|---|---|---|---|---|---|---|
| | | | | | | 1 |
| 2 | 3 | 4 | 5 | 6 | 7 | 8 |
| 9 | 10 | 11 | 12 | 13 | 14 | 15 |
| 16 | 17 | 18 | 19 | 20 | 21 | 22 |
| 23 | 24 | 25 | 26 | 27 | 28 | 29 |

### MARCH

| S | M | T | W | T | F | S |
|---|---|---|---|---|---|---|
| 1 | 2 | 3 | 4 | 5 | 6 | 7 |
| 8 | 9 | 10 | 11 | 12 | 13 | 14 |
| 15 | 16 | 17 | 18 | 19 | 20 | 21 |
| 22 | 23 | 24 | 25 | 26 | 27 | 28 |
| 29 | 30 | 31 | | | | |

### APRIL

| S | M | T | W | T | F | S |
|---|---|---|---|---|---|---|
| | | | 1 | 2 | 3 | 4 |
| 5 | 6 | 7 | 8 | 9 | 10 | 11 |
| 12 | 13 | 14 | 15 | 16 | 17 | 18 |
| 19 | 20 | 21 | 22 | 23 | 24 | 25 |
| 26 | 27 | 28 | 29 | 30 | | |

### MAY

| S | M | T | W | T | F | S |
|---|---|---|---|---|---|---|
| 31 | | | | | 1 | 2 |
| 3 | 4 | 5 | 6 | 7 | 8 | 9 |
| 10 | 11 | 12 | 13 | 14 | 15 | 16 |
| 17 | 18 | 19 | 20 | 21 | 22 | 23 |
| 24 | 25 | 26 | 27 | 28 | 29 | 30 |

### JUNE

| S | M | T | W | T | F | S |
|---|---|---|---|---|---|---|
| | 1 | 2 | 3 | 4 | 5 | 6 |
| 7 | 8 | 9 | 10 | 11 | 12 | 13 |
| 14 | 15 | 16 | 17 | 18 | 19 | 20 |
| 21 | 22 | 23 | 24 | 25 | 26 | 27 |
| 28 | 29 | 30 | | | | |

## 2020 NORTHERN HEMISPHERE MOON PHASES

**JULY**

| S | M | T | W | T | F | S |
|---|---|---|---|---|---|---|
| | | | 1 | 2 | 3 | 4 |
| 5 | 6 | 7 | 8 | 9 | 10 | 11 |
| 12 | 13 | 14 | 15 | 16 | 17 | 18 |
| 19 | 20 | 21 | 22 | 23 | 24 | 25 |
| 26 | 27 | 28 | 29 | 30 | 31 | |

**AUGUST**

| S | M | T | W | T | F | S |
|---|---|---|---|---|---|---|
| 30 | 31 | | | | | 1 |
| 2 | 3 | 4 | 5 | 6 | 7 | 8 |
| 9 | 10 | 11 | 12 | 13 | 14 | 15 |
| 16 | 17 | 18 | 19 | 20 | 21 | 22 |
| 23 | 24 | 25 | 26 | 27 | 28 | 29 |

**SEPTEMBER**

| S | M | T | W | T | F | S |
|---|---|---|---|---|---|---|
| | | 1 | 2 | 3 | 4 | 5 |
| 6 | 7 | 8 | 9 | 10 | 11 | 12 |
| 13 | 14 | 15 | 16 | 17 | 18 | 19 |
| 20 | 21 | 22 | 23 | 24 | 25 | 26 |
| 27 | 28 | 29 | 30 | | | |

**OCTOBER**

| S | M | T | W | T | F | S |
|---|---|---|---|---|---|---|
| | | | | 1 | 2 | 3 |
| 4 | 5 | 6 | 7 | 8 | 9 | 10 |
| 11 | 12 | 13 | 14 | 15 | 16 | 17 |
| 18 | 19 | 20 | 21 | 22 | 23 | 24 |
| 25 | 26 | 27 | 28 | 29 | 30 | 31 |

**NOVEMBER**

| S | M | T | W | T | F | S |
|---|---|---|---|---|---|---|
| 1 | 2 | 3 | 4 | 5 | 6 | 7 |
| 8 | 9 | 10 | 11 | 12 | 13 | 14 |
| 15 | 16 | 17 | 18 | 19 | 20 | 21 |
| 22 | 23 | 24 | 25 | 26 | 27 | 28 |
| 29 | 30 | | | | | |

**DECEMBER**

| S | M | T | W | T | F | S |
|---|---|---|---|---|---|---|
| | | 1 | 2 | 3 | 4 | 5 |
| 6 | 7 | 8 | 9 | 10 | 11 | 12 |
| 13 | 14 | 15 | 16 | 17 | 18 | 19 |
| 20 | 21 | 22 | 23 | 24 | 25 | 26 |
| 27 | 28 | 29 | 30 | 31 | | |

○ New moon ● Full moon

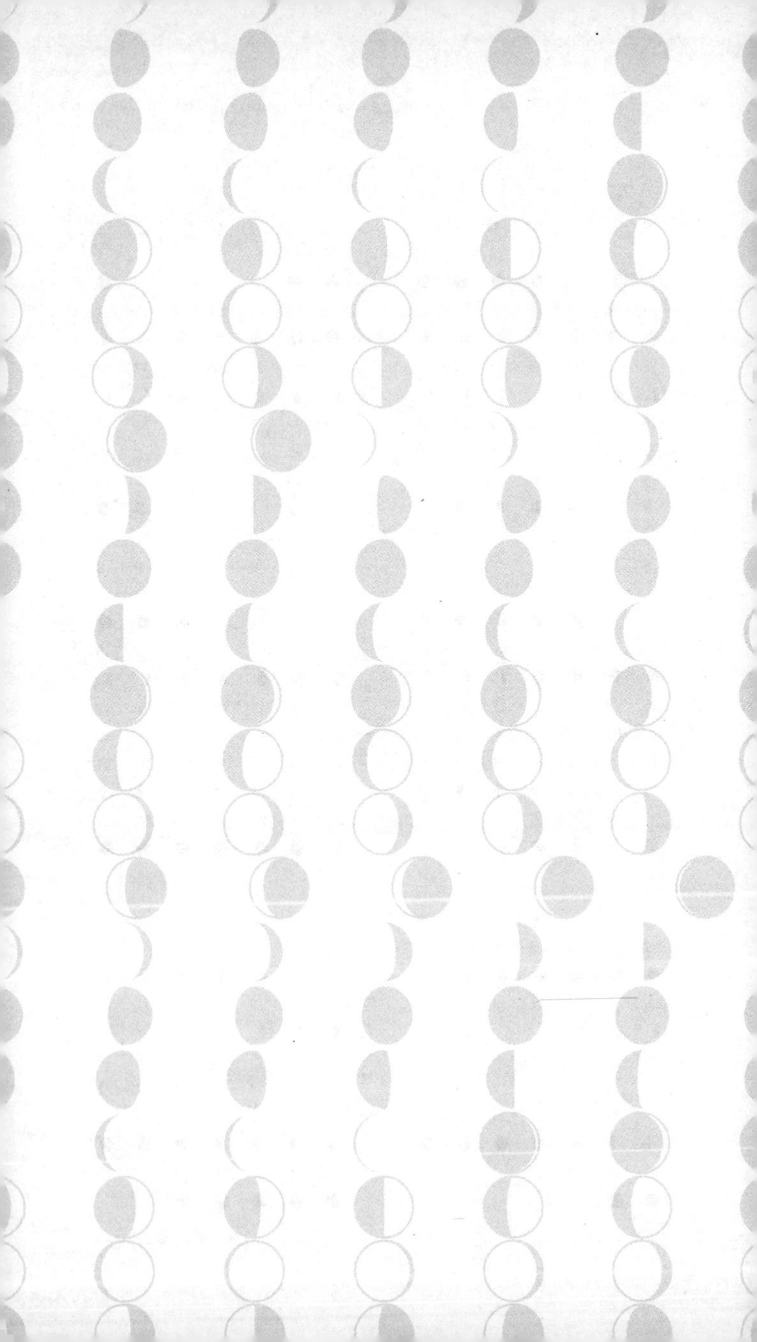

# Cancer in love

You are a particularly independent individual who is likely to be selective about who you spend long-term time with. In this chapter you can check out your compatibility with other sun signs. Remember that we are all complex individuals, so the more you know about someone's astrological birth chart the better you can determine your compatibility. Consider having your astrological birth chart compared with that of a partner, friend or family member, as the compatibility – known as synastry in astrology – goes even deeper than a comparison of sun signs, although this is a good place to begin.

## Cancer with Aries

You are both cardinal signs, which means you are both strong characters, so there has to be give and take or one of you will feel you are playing second fiddle to the other. Your Cancerian sensitivity can feel overshadowed by the Aries dominant approach, and Aries can feel invalidated by Cancerian mood swings, especially when you are usually such a supportive sign.

If you can establish a solid platform of mutual respect this match can work. Some might say it is a difficult match, but it largely depends on how willing you are to work on your relationship and whether there is other compatibility in your chart, such as compatible moon signs.

## Cancer with Taurus

Cancer is a water sign and is inherently intuitive, instinctive, caring and nurturing. Taurus is an earth sign and practical, methodical and sensual and enjoys the good things in life. Your mutual interest is likely to cross over in areas such as nurturance, caring for each other's well-being and a predisposition for good food and drink. However, your fundamental approach to life is very different and therefore could signal disagreements about essential daily matters.

## Cancer with Gemini

The Cancerian personality is gentle, sensitive and introspective, yet underneath your inner resourcefulness and ability to stand your ground may be quite a surprise to Gemini. You are a diligent and strong character, and once your mind is made up there is little that will change it. The combination of an earth sign with a water sign could pose difficulties once the initial attraction wears off, as you need different qualities from each other. You need support and stability and Gemini needs freedom of movement and independence despite being a loyal character.

## Cancer with Cancer

You are both cardinal signs and thus are both strong characters.

While this may initially present as the ideal twinning, too much of a good thing can be a setback. You are both highly sensitive and intuitive, and unless you have learned to manage your sensitivity and psychic abilities you can easily become confused and misread each other's thoughts and actions. You may tend to see life through each other's eyes, not seeing where you begin and where your partner begins. Blurred lines between you can lead to confusion, but you can make a good pairing if you are conscious about your abilities and tendency to see deeper into each other's actions and talk frequently and constructively about the best way forward in real terms.

## Cancer with Leo

Leo is ruled by the sun, the centre of the solar system, so Leos like to be the centre of attention; the sun really does shine from them! Cancer would need to initially take the back seat in this relationship or else the Leo will not feel they can shine. The quieter Cancerian personality may play this role in the beginning, but as both these signs are super strong willed this combo can lead to a battle unless both are conscious of each other's boundaries and respectful of each other's power.

## Cancer with Virgo

The earthy Virgo will initially appeal as a sensual lover, someone with whom you can feel empathy. You may also enjoy the sense of safety, security and care emanating from Virgo. Virgo will appreciate your apparent emotional intelligence, tenderness and compassion. These signs can certainly gain much from each other and can be mutually supportive, but both can be

cantankerous and the Cancerian character will undoubtedly wish to take control over certain issues, which is something Virgo may need to adapt to.

## Cancer with Libra

This is a double cardinal match, so while both these sun signs appear on the surface to be soft, gentle characters both will wish to take the lead. They will do so in different ways: you will want to be heard emotionally and be emotionally fulfilled, while the Libra sun sign will want to be heard and respected and find peace and harmony. As both signs can be indecisive and constantly looking for emotional and mental support from each other, this match can tend to fall flat unless both partners make a conscious effort to constantly support each other. This can be tiring, especially when both are indecisive and looking for personal fulfilment from the other rather than from themselves. If you have strong air in your chart and the Libran strong water, this combination could work.

## Cancer with Scorpio

Two water signs make for a passionate, emotional and intense relationship. However, both partners risk feeling overwhelmed by the other, so it's important in this relationship to maintain healthy boundaries and focus on self-care as otherwise it can result in co-dependency. That aside, this is one of the best matches for the Cancerian individual as the two signs are on the same page emotionally; you have similar outlooks in life as you are both intuitive and passionate about your activities. This

relationship goes much deeper than many others, so if you are willing to explore the wonders of love it can be fulfilling.

## Cancer with Sagittarius

It's a case of opposites attracting: you will admire the fire and excitement offered by the Sagittarian, and the Sagittarian will be intrigued and seduced by your tenderness and allure. However, the Cancerian water sign tends to pour cold water on the fire of the Sagittarian, despite initial attraction on both parts. In other words you, driven principally by emotions, can overwhelm the get-up-and-go of the Sagittarian, seemingly clipping their wings, albeit unintentionally. Unless, that is, care is taken to understand the other: the Cancerian is principally a caring, nurturing person; the Sagittarian principally an outgoing adventurer. Clearly these two people are very different. Embrace your differences and allow them to complement one other and you have a good match.

## Cancer with Capricorn

This is a case of opposites attracting, although you have more common ground than initially meets the eye. You are both cardinal signs, which means you are both strong characters and therefore understand each other's approach life: it's direct and often goal oriented. The earthiness of the Capricorn will represent safety and security to Cancer and your elusiveness and sensitivity can represent a feeling of completion for Capricorn, who is essentially practical, reasonable and intellectual. This is a match for partnership, as long as both are willing to give in to the other on occasion and in equal measures.

## Cancer with Aquarius

Cancerians look for safety, security and emotional contentment in a partnership. You are unlikely to find this in the Aquarian, who is essentially quirky, restless and eccentric and can be unreliable, even if unintentionally. While this match may be enticing and even exciting at first, both partners are likely to feel unfulfilled by the other unless there are other indicators in your mutual astrology charts that suggest compatibility such as a sun–moon compatibility. The Cancerian may feel unsupported emotionally by the Aquarian and the Aquarian emotionally beleaguered by the Cancerian. As companions and friends, however, this can be a light-hearted, fun relationship as both approach life with such different attitudes and can teach the other much in life.

## Cancer with Pisces

This is a recipe for success as you are both water signs and have an innate understanding of each other. You are both intuitive, sensitive and tender partners, although the Pisces tendency for daydreaming may be foreign to the more centred, strong Cancerian. You will wish to take the lead in this relationship, so Pisces must avoid playing the victim-martyr role. Both signs are complex so must give each other space for introspective phases. This is, however, a naturally mutually supportive partnership and can be positive for long-term commitment.

# Mercury and Venus retrograde periods in 2020

The dates listed in this section indicate when both Mercury and Venus will be retrograde in 2020. A planet is termed 'retrograde' when it appears to be going backwards around the sun from our point of view here on earth. Of course, no planet actually goes retrograde – it's an optical illusion – but these phases do exhibit certain characteristics.

During the Mercury retrograde phase communications can tend to be a little more difficult than during the 'direct' phase, when the planet has a forwards motion. Travel may also be delayed or cancelled. However, the Mercury retrograde phase can be an excellent time for reviewing your circumstances, for reassessing where you are in life and for re-organising your various duties. Plan to take a slightly slower lane in life, such as a holiday, and don't expect communications to be perfect and for computers to run without a hitch.

During the Venus retrograde phase you might find that relationships are less likely to forge ahead under blue skies, and that sometimes when a Venus retrograde phase coincides with a Mercury retrograde communications may be complex or easily predisposed to arguments. The plus side is that Venus retrograde

phases provide an ideal time to take things a little more slowly, to be less demanding on yourself and others within your relationships and practise compassion and kindness. Patience is truly a virtue during the Mercury and Venus retrograde periods.

## Mercury retrograde phases in 2020:

17 February to 9 March

18 June to 11 July

14 October to 2 November

## Venus retrograde phase in 2020:

13 May to 23 June

# The year ahead for Cancer

Affirmation for the year: *'I embrace change!'*

Uranus at the zenith of your chart will provide a sense of excitement but also of change. You like to feel you are settled, especially in the domestic realm, yet developments this year could prise you out of your shell and into new territory. It's important to embrace change, because if you refuse the sound of your own wheels spinning could take you nowhere fast.

The alignment of Jupiter, Saturn and Pluto in your seventh house of partnerships suggests that in 2020 you will place a great deal of focus on collaborations, both in your personal life such as a love partnership or marriage and in your professional life – think joint business ventures.

The first two quarters of the year will require focus on self-care and nurturance of others. Once the moon's north node leaves your sign in early May, your attention will switch from matters to do with self-nurture and the nurture of others and will lean more towards networking, communications and work.

Mars traversing your adventure zone mid-year will make adventure appeal to you, especially in the second half of the year, and this may take the shape of study, travel, spiritual activity or even legal matters that will open new paths for you. However, until early September your career, status and general direction could be the true focus. With five planets retrograde from 23 June until 12 July, these three weeks will be an ideal time to plan and strategise rather than to take action if possible.

The conjunction of Jupiter and Pluto on 30 June will spotlight your true feelings about the depth of change you may contemplate long term. The ongoing Venus–Saturn trine early in July will show alternative options, and while the most adventurous course of action may appeal to you you may be inclined to stick with the tried and trusted.

There is no rush this year with long-term decisions; in fact, impulsive decisions could be your downfall. If you feel you must take decisive action try to set new wheels in motion towards the end of July, and if possible after or on the Cancerian new moon on 20 July, which could truly launch you into new professional and/or personal collaborations. Be careful at this time to ensure you have all the facts at your fingertips.

## Health

This year's Cancerians are generally divided into two groups: those born before the first week of July and those born afterwards. The latter will experience the most focus and potential change healthwise this year. For you, it will be important to focus on the changing face of your daily routine and to keep on top of health and wellness to ensure you don't run out of steam. You may be particularly focused on health early in the year, in early April, the end of June and September and in mid-November and December.

For all Cancerians, the period from April to early August will place considerable focus on health and well-being, and especially from mid-May to early July when energy levels may require attention. Ask yourself if you've taken on too much, and if stress is a factor. If so, this will be your cue to slow down and consider new ways to nurture both yourself and others. Concerted effort in the health field will see your energy levels rally, at the very least by the end of the year when you should enjoy a sense of renewed vitality.

## Finances

Whether your focus is on personal partnerships, that is, your marriage and home life, or on your work and furtherance of career and status, you should reap the rewards by the end of August for a lot of your hard work. With the sun and Mercury in prudent Virgo, favourably aspecting Uranus, this is a time when you could make advantageous financial decisions. As with any decision it's important to avoid impulsiveness; detailed research will be necessary.

September looks to be a fortunate time financially, when you should see your coffers refilled. However, you may be prone to overspending at this time, so avoid allowing any leaks in the financial bucket to persist.

## Home life

Because a considerable amount of your energy will be expended on nurture and care of yourself and others, until May at least,

and your relationships will see key changes, your home life will be the centre of operations. Therefore, it's important you feel secure and stable in that area. If you feel the opposite, it's time to make the necessary changes.

The full moon in your home sector on 7 May should encourage you to take action where you may have previously been reluctant to do so. This will coincide with the transit of the moon's north node into Gemini, providing the sense that communications, meeting and trips will be beneficial in moving the energy around at home to better suit your needs and those of others.

The sun in your home sector in October and November followed by Venus in your domestic realm in December will provide you with a wonderful sense of completion and relaxation at the end of the year.

## Love

Three of the six eclipses in 2020 will be across the relationship sectors in your chart, suggesting this is the year when a great deal can change in your business and personal partnerships. If love has thrown you a curve ball in recent times, prepare for that to change! The lunar eclipse on 11 January will provide a good idea of the intensity of developments to come in your love life this year. The eclipse season from June to July indicates considerable changes, perhaps due to your partner's circumstances rather than your own, and a change in your attitude to each other.

For some Cancerians the developments will take you out of a rut. For singles, there will be new partnerships to consider.

There may be a tendency to hang on to the past, so self-nurturing and embracing your willingness to live and learn through your relationships will certainly help you should you be reluctant to change, especially from mid-May to the end of June.

In July you will relish the opportunity to enjoy romance and a holiday or a relaxing retreat, or simply the wish to learn more about love and life so you can progress with a deeper understanding of love.

Uranus at the zenith of your chart all year suggests your status may change, and this can include your status from single to married or vice versa. In mid-August you may need to make a tough call, but if you trust your intuition and the sense of destiny a particular partnership has your decisions won't be difficult.

## Career

The focus this year is so strongly on partnerships that if you collaborate with a business partner there will be changes in the structure of your career and work scenario.

Key developments concerning a business or personal partner are likely to occur early in the year, in mid-year and then once again towards the end of the year, although the entire year is likely to entail developments that will put you in a very different place by 2021.

Uranus in your 10th house of career will contribute to the sense of change. This may simply come out of restlessness or be due to changes in your marital status. At various points in the year you may find that the way you share your assets, duties and resources will affect how you decide to move your career forward; care must be taken with these decisions.

Late February could see considerable change in your career, as you embrace a work ethic that could bring you more stability.

The period from 14–16 July will add more incentive to commit to someone in business or to an exciting plan, so keep your eyes peeled if you're looking for new opportunities.

# Cancer 2020 diary

It's likely you are most familiar with the study of your sun sign via your horoscope, and horoscopes are plentiful nowadays for daily guidance. In *Your Horoscope for 2020: Cancer* you can find out what's coming up for you personally, which is important because we don't all react the same way to the same phenomena. For example, when the sun is in your own sign it can prove particularly motivational and is a great time to get ahead with projects that resonate with your self-esteem, gut instincts and bigger-picture motivation. In the same way, when planets from Mercury to Pluto pass through your sun sign there will be particular influences that are explained in the diary; it'll be for you to take the initiative and instigate plans and projects that resonate with the prevailing mood.

Astrology isn't a phenomenon that happens to you: you need to take action! When the sun passes through Leo from 23 July to 22 August Leos will tend to feel revitalised, energised and motivated so this is a great time to get things rolling. But for Scorpios this phase may not be the same; there will be more focus on career and direction and hard work, as opposed to simply

feeling energised. *Your Horoscope for 2020: Cancer* will provide invaluable direction to help you find your best-case scenario during various phases of the year and know the pitfalls to avoid.

## Interplanetary aspects

Astrologers study the movements of planets in relation to each other; the measurements are in degrees, minutes and seconds. These measurements focus on patterns and particular aspects such as the angles between the planets, the sun and other celestial objects. This book includes mention of the aspects between the sun and the planets; the terminology is explained below.

The angles the planets and the sun make to one another have meaning in astrology. For example, a 'trine' aspect (120 degree angle) can be considered beneficial for the progress of your plans; a 'square' aspect (90 degree angle) can present as a challenge depending on your own attitude to challenges and obstacles. By carefully choosing dates for the fruition of your plans you will be able to move forward with knowledge of the cosmic influences that can help your progress.

**Conjunction:** when a celestial object is at the same degree as another celestial object and therefore aligned from our point of view here on earth. This can intensify the dynamics between the celestial objects and earth.

**Opposition:** when a planet is opposite another at a 180 degree angle. This can intensify the interplanetary dynamics.

**Quincunx:** a 150 degree angle can present a hurdle to be overcome.

**Semi-sextile:** a 30 degree angle can be a peaceful, harmonious influence or can facilitate the flow of energy between planetary influences.

**Sextile:** a 60 degree angle can be a peaceful, harmonious influence or can facilitate the flow of energy between planetary influences.

**Square:** a 90 degree angle can be a challenging aspect; however, as some people get going when the going gets tough it can lead to a breakthrough.

**Trine:** a 120 degree angle can be a peaceful, harmonious influence or can facilitate the flow of energy between planetary influences.

## Retrogrades

Planets can appear to go backwards from our point of view here on earth; this is known as a retrograde phase. The most well-known retrograde phases are those of Mercury, although several other planets also turn retrograde; these phases are mentioned in the diary. Retrograde phases can be a good time to assimilate, consolidate and integrate recent developments, although traditionally they are associated with delays, a slow down or a difficult process. For example, a Mercury retrograde phase is often aligned with difficult communications or traffic snarls, yet it can be an excellent time to integrate events and to consolidate, review and re-order your ideas. The influences of Mercury and Venus retrograde phases on your sun sign are explained in the diary pages and on page 37.

## Eclipses, new moons and full moons

Just as retrograde phases can have an impact on your life, so too can eclipses, new moons and full moons. All of these events will be explained and listed in the diary, enabling you to plan ahead with the full knowledge that you're moving in synchronicity with the sun, moon and stars.

# JANUARY

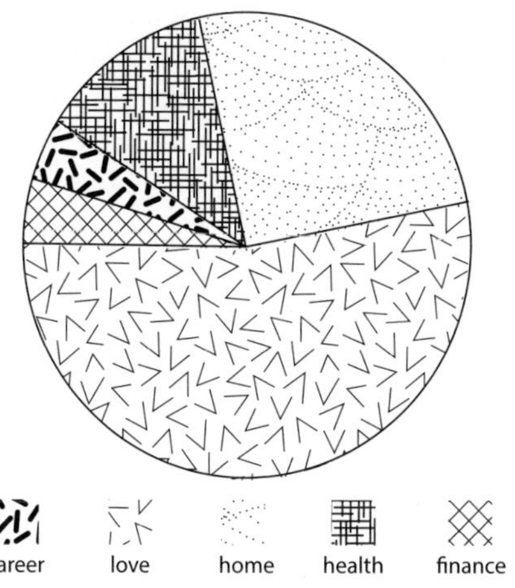


***Notes:*** The pie charts such as the one above listed for each month show energy distribution according to the stars for the month ahead. If you wish to make changes in the areas of your finances, health, career, love or home and you see there is a large amount of energy in that sector in the chart, your endeavours should succeed as long as you have prepared well in advance. The charts also show which areas will potentially have the most focus in your life during the month.

The moon sign listed for each day's entry in the diary is the position of the moon at the end of the day in Greenwich Mean Time (GMT).

## 1 January

A change of routine will feel exciting and well deserved. You'll enjoy giving full rein to your dreamy, inspired side and doing something different to celebrate 1 January. You may be ready to make a commitment to a bold plan this year, beginning today! ***Moon in Pisces***.

## 2 January

A business or personal partner will have news for you, especially if you were born at the end of June. A trip or visit should be enjoyable. A work decision or the need to get back to work will mean a change of routine. This is a good day to boost health and well-being. ***Moon enters Aries.***

## 3 January

An outgoing, upbeat approach to your work and social life will bear fruit. If you must return to work soon pave the way ahead with good intentions. A reunion should be enjoyable this weekend. ***Moon in Aries.***

## 4 January

You'll enjoy the chance to focus on your own well-being, and to boost your health through a visit somewhere beautiful and the chance to indulge your closest relationships. This is a good day for organising yourself in preparation for work and domestic chores. ***Moon enters Taurus.***

## 5 January

You'll enjoy a change of routine and the chance to get down to work with your various chores and duties around the house and garden. There is a therapeutic quality to the day that you'll relish. Holidaying crabs will enjoy indulging in upbeat activities. ***Moon in Taurus.***

## 6 January

You'll appreciate the opportunity to collaborate either with a colleague, employer or partner. You have the same goals at the moment and will enjoy being adventurous with them. A social event will be enjoyable. ***Moon in Taurus.***

## 7 January

Some lovely developments are possible. This is fundamentally a romantic day; art, music, love and candlelight will all appeal to you so organise a date or a treat. You may reach an important agreement in your personal life or at work but must be clear about your aims. ***Moon in Gemini.***

## 8 January

Agreements and contracts could be signed; you may be ready to move forward in exciting and practical ways. A get together will feel special. If you're single you may meet someone who seems familiar. Couples could reach an important romantic turning point. Financial matters could be decisive, so ensure you are happy with the terms or plan to make changes to them. ***Moon in Gemini.***

## 9 January

In the run-up to the Cancer eclipse life may feel a little intense. Nevertheless, it's a good day for important decisions, especially those concerning your personal life and joint financial or work agreements. ***Moon in Cancer.***

## 10 January

Tomorrow's partial eclipse in Cancer will clarify where you stand with a personal or work matter. For some, this eclipse will spotlight either your own health and well-being or that of someone close. Take your time with decisions and do your research. A trip or get together may be more significant than meets the eye.

## 11 January

The Cancer eclipse will spotlight key work and health matters. This is a good day for a health appointment. You'll enjoy an upbeat and outgoing feeling once the moon is in Leo this evening if not before, and being active with friends and beautifying your home and environment.

## 12 January

Trust your gut instincts if you're unsure about a decision. A partnership may take up much of your time and energy, so ensure you are happy with the direction your joint decisions take you or plan to make changes. Romance could skyrocket. ***Moon in Leo.***

## 13 January

Key news or meetings could be pivotal for a partnership or relationship. This is a good day for meetings, although there may be a great deal to decide upon. You may need to take responsibility for serious decisions, but you must be methodical and avoid rushing. ***Moon enters Virgo.***

## 14 January

Today's Virgo moon will help you make key decisions, especially in relation to home, work and finances. This is a good day for planning, strategy and getting ahead with your favourite interests. Holidaying crabs will enjoy boosting health and well-being.

## 15 January

A surprise visit or impromptu invitation may be pleasant, so be open to a little spontaneity. A visit or romantic tryst will be enjoyable or even therapeutic, so go ahead and plan a treat. ***Moon enters Libra.***

## 16 January

Today's moon in Libra will prompt a need for calm and balance, especially in your communications and at home. Take the time to slow down when you can and enjoy some peace in your own environment.

## 17 January

A partner or work colleague may have news that seems unusual or unexpected; try to look outside the square to understand a different perspective. Your deeper feelings are likely to emerge and you may be surprised by your emotions; take your time to process them. ***Moon enters Scorpio.***

## 18 January

A surprise or impromptu get together may lead to a new understanding of yourself or of someone else. A group, friend or organisation may be in a changeable situation that affects you. You're a sensitive character, so avoid being affected by others' circumstances without losing empathy. ***Moon in Scorpio.***

## 19 January

This is a great day to boost your health and well-being and your family and interpersonal dynamics. If you have been overworking, aim for a break. If you are artistic or musical, being creative will soothe the soul. Romance could blossom. ***Moon in Scorpio.***

## 20 January

You may be aware that a business or personal partnership is entering a new era due to someone's behaviour or simply due to circumstances. Look for original ways to interrelate. A fresh understanding could begin to develop. ***Moon in Sagittarius.***

## 21 January

Talks should go well, especially if you look for different ways to approach someone with whom you work or live. You'll enjoy branching out and trying new ideas and plans. This is an innovative time, so let your imagination run free but be practical. ***Moon in Sagittarius.***

## 22 January

There is a therapeutic quality to events. Teaching, study, research and generally broadening your horizons will appeal, and your efforts to improve circumstances should be successful. Avoid being overly sensitive to criticism. ***Moon enters Capricorn.***

## 23 January

Talks and meetings, negotiations and news may be fast paced so you must focus on getting the right end of the stick, especially if you are under pressure. Someone may surprise you as they interpret both your and their own circumstances differently. Aim for clarity. ***Moon in Capricorn.***

## 24 January

Tomorrow's Aquarian new moon will shed light on a shared project or a relationship. Be prepared to see things in a new light and to be adventurous. For some, this new moon phase will be about re-inventing a relationship or an agreement. You'll enjoy getting together with a business or personal partner. Romance could flourish.

## 25 January

The current new moon phase is good for communications and improving relationships, so take the initiative and organise a get together. Romance could flourish. A family outing or news from someone close should be motivational. Avoid impulsiveness. ***Moon in Aquarius.***

## 26 January

You'll enjoy a get together and the sense of collaboration it brings you. However, it seems not everyone can see eye to eye so avoid arguments; they could spiral. ***Moon in Pisces.***

## 27 January

This is a good day for get togethers, both in your personal life and at an activity you enjoy such as a spiritual endeavour. Romance could sizzle. You'll appreciate the chance to let your imagination run free with art, music and dance. Avoid forgetfulness and idealism by keeping your feet on the ground. ***Moon in Pisces.***

## 28 January

You are a sensitive character and today's Pisces moon may bring your vulnerability out. Be careful to avoid needless arguments, and enjoy a break. A trip will be uplifting. You may tend to be absent-minded so make sure you focus, especially at work.

## 29 January

You should hear good news, either from a partner or at work. Some Cancerians may hear good health news that will encourage you to keep on the track you're on. This is a good day for collaborations and partnerships, so aim to co-operate and you'll enjoy your day all the more. ***Moon enters Aries.***

## 30 January

You'll enjoy spending time with someone you love. This is a good day for talks as you'll feel dynamic, but you must avoid trying to push for answers or results and taking other people's problems personally. ***Moon in Aries.***

## 31 January

This is a good day for talks and negotiations and setting solid plans in motion, especially at work and with a partner. You may be ready to make a commitment. Avoid making assumptions and pushing for a result; be patient. ***Moon in Aries.***

# FEBRUARY

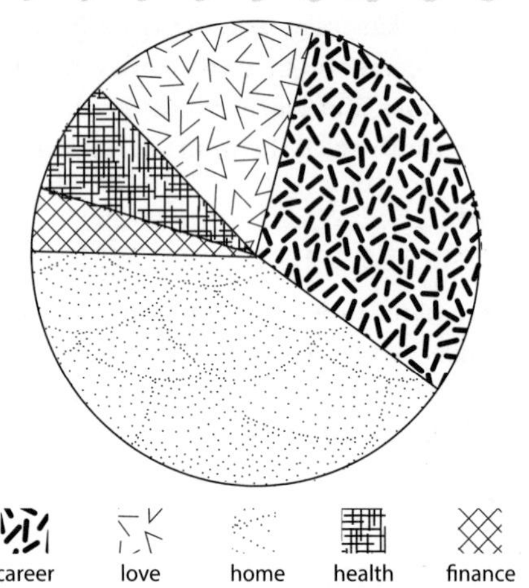


## 1 February

With authority comes responsibility, and your work life may demand you seize the reins. If you're looking for work it's a good time to circulate your resume. If you're looking for a promotion, suggest a talk with your employer. A favourite activity will be appealing. ***Moon enters Taurus.***

## 2 February

This is a lovely day for get togethers and collaborations. If you're working it should be a busy and productive day, but you may need to focus that little bit more than usual. A trip or a visit somewhere beautiful will be enjoyable. Romance could blossom. ***Moon in Taurus.***

## 3 February

Your ventures could blossom, so put your energy into work. If you're looking for a commitment at work or in your personal life ask for one now; you are likely to get what you want. You will gain direction if you have been undergoing negotiations or legal matters. ***Moon in Gemini.***

## 4 February

The Gemini moon will bring your inquisitive nature out. You may wish to look behind the scenes at your ventures and find out more about how you truly feel about circumstances. Avoid letting out a secret you are guarding for someone. Keep communications on an even keel to avoid disputes.

## 5 February

Discussions could open a door to a better mutual understanding, but if the understanding does not transpire to what you'd hoped for it's important you acknowledge to yourself that you feel undervalued. Someone will prove surprisingly helpful. ***Moon in Gemini.***

## 6 February

This is a good day for discussions and deepening relationships. You may enjoy art, music and dance and feel inspired and creative; romance could blossom. If discussions at work are unclear or you receive mixed messages, find out more. ***Moon in Cancer.***

## 7 February

You'll appreciate the chance to put your efforts into changes you've been working on. Your efforts could improve relationships in those areas where you need the change the most, at work or at home. This is a great day for work meetings and to discuss important decisions. ***Moon in Cancer.***

## 8 February

You'll appreciate the opportunity to be more active, sporty or outgoing this weekend. Someone you look after or care for may ask for your help, which you'll enjoy giving. A health or beauty treat will appeal; it'll be relaxing and boost self-esteem. ***Moon in Leo.***

## 9 February

The Leo full moon will shine a light on your relationships, interactions and communications and on ways to improve these areas. A new digital device may improve communications. For some, the full moon will spotlight finances and the need to be adventurous about finding the best way to save and budget.

## 10 February

News from a group or organisation such as your employer will be a focus. You may be asked to help or will need to ask for help yourself. A surprising development may present as a struggle but will eventually have a healing effect. A healthy outdoors activity will appeal. ***Moon in Virgo.***

## 11 February

The Virgo moon will have a constructive, productive effect, enabling you to complete your various chores and be practical with paperwork and domestic matters. Be patient with laborious tasks; you will soon get through them.

## 12 February

Today's Libran moon will help you digest various events that have recently occurred. If you have felt vulnerable you should regain composure and balance. You will get perspective when you consider how best to gain proportion and harmony into your life. Take time out if possible. ***Moon in Libra.***

## 13 February

This is a good day for collaborative efforts. When you feel you're at loggerheads with someone often the best way forward is to talk, but if fundamental differences revolve around conflicting values then talks can stall. Try small steps first to come to agreement. ***Moon in Libra.***

## 14 February

Happy St Valentine's Day! You'll enjoy the general atmosphere of the day, around which there is a dynamic feeling; work could also progress and romance certainly blossom. However, you may have different plans for the day and evening so ensure you reach a mutual agreement. ***Moon in Scorpio.***

## 15 February

This is a good day to make agreements, at work or in your personal life. You'll enjoy an activity you both love, and planning ahead for travel or for study and self-improvement. It's a good day to make a commitment to someone; it's likely to stick. ***Moon in Scorpio.***

## 16 February

The moon will encourage you to be outgoing and adventurous. You'll enjoy meeting with like-minded people and socialising. If you have recently argued with someone, this is a good day for making up. ***Moon in Sagittarius.***

## 17 February

Mercury turns retrograde, which will highlight your thoughts regarding your beliefs, partnership and bigger picture plans. Try to get loose ends and paperwork tied up. If you're travelling, plan ahead to avoid delays. Be careful with communications to avoid misunderstandings. ***Moon in Sagittarius.***

## 18 February

You may need to review some arrangements, either work agreements or to do with a partner. You'll have the time to reconsider your circumstances, so avoid rushing decisions. ***Moon enters Capricorn.***

## 19 February

As the sun enters Pisces you should enjoy a more inspired four weeks, especially within your partnerships and your activities. You will wish to give your imagination wings through the arts, spirituality, dance and music. The moon in Capricorn will help keep your feet on the ground.

## 20 February

There may be super ideal elements in your day, although some aspects may feel frustrating as it may be difficult to pin someone down and gain traction with your ventures. Be patient. Romance and your favourite activities could blossom. ***Moon in Capricorn.***

## 21 February

You may hear unexpected news at work, in your personal life or regarding study, a legal matter or spiritual beliefs. If you're planning a trip it could feel liberating. Avoid impulsiveness and rash decisions; you may regret them. ***Moon in Aquarius.***

## 22 February

You may be surprised by developments. A venture may take a new turn, and someone may surprise you with a trip somewhere beautiful. Don't be afraid to step into fresh territory. ***Moon in Aquarius.***

## 23 February

Tomorrow's Pisces new moon signals a new chapter in a venture or shared area of your life such as finances, duties or responsibilities. An inspiring learning curve could open doors for you. Be willing to indulge in and celebrate what makes your heart sing.

## 24 February

The new moon is inspiring, so it is an excellent time to align your hopes, beliefs and wishes with your actions to find more meaning and purpose. If you have undergone arguments, find ways to reconcile with your viewpoints and move ahead peacefully.

## 25 February

You can truly steam ahead with your various projects, so stride along optimistically. For some progress will be at work; for others in your various interests. Collaborations, especially, should go well. Avoid impulsiveness. ***Moon in Aries.***

## 26 February

Key news, a trip or talks could truly move you forward at work, so take the initiative to get in touch with people you know could help you with your projects. Today's developments could revolve around a learning curve and the chance to boost your experience and knowledge through study and adventure. Be bold. ***Moon in Aries.***

## 27 February

Today's Aries moon will keep you busy. Remain grounded and practical if are a little at odds with someone, as you may feel restless and some communications may be tense. Avoid arguments, as these are likely to spiral over the next two days. ***Moon in Aries.***

## 28 February

The Venus–Pluto tension may lead to intense emotions, either in yourself or in someone you must co-operate with. A little tension may be exciting in a passionate relationship, but if you encounter a disagreement avoid allowing it to escalate. You could truly excel with your projects but you must avoid power struggles. ***Moon in Taurus.***

## 29 February

It's a leap year! An unexpected invitation to an event or a lovely get together or activity will add a little variety to your day, so organise something different if you haven't already. ***Moon in Taurus.***

# MARCH

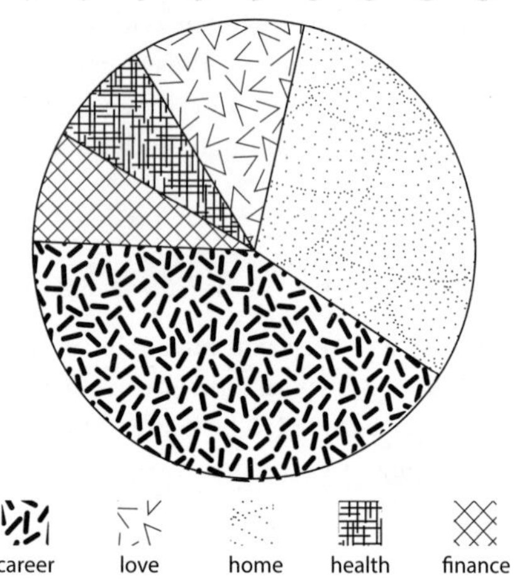


## 1 March

You'll appreciate relaxing. A trip to the ocean or a favourite past-time or get together with someone you love will appeal. Romance will be a priority but you may need to be patient. Working crabs will be busy and productive but you must make time to relax. Avoid ruffled feathers; be practical. ***Moon in Taurus.***

## 2 March

Mercury retrograde in dreamy Pisces and the moon in Gemini means you'll enjoy being imaginative and mixing with artistic and creative people. It's a good day for meditation and yoga, exercise and work progress. ***Moon in Gemini.***

## 3 March

An agreement or an arrangement you are working towards could come to fruition. If you discover that someone's commitment to you or a project is lacking, it may be time to discuss your alternative options. You must avoid locking horns with someone with whom you have to collaborate. ***Moon in Gemini.***

## 4 March

You may manage a breakthrough with a particular agreement, arrangement or relationship, so take the initiative to make amends if you have argued or to make progress with talks. ***Moon enters Cancer.***

## 5 March

You'll appreciate the calming influence of today's moon in Cancer. You may enjoy a reunion or the chance to reconnect with someone with whom you must share duties or responsibilities. Trust your intuition. This is a good day for spiritual and insightful, creative and intuitive work.

## 6 March

Venus in Taurus will put the focus firmly on practicalities over the next four weeks, and you'll notice your desire for more stability at work and in your relationships and your past-times. To gain a stronger foundation you may need to first undergo some changes. A friend or organisation may help. ***Moon enters Leo.***

## 7 March

This is a good day for talking. You'll appreciate being able to make practical arrangements with someone close, be this a business or marital partner or a friend, family member or colleague. You may hear good news from a partner or in relation to work, a shared duty or finances. ***Moon in Leo.***

## 8 March

Romance could blossom, so organise a beautiful event such as a visit to the beach or a sumptuous restaurant. An artistic, spiritual or musical event will appeal. You may be ready to try something new or to meet a new social circle. If you're working you may be unexpectedly busy. ***Moon in Leo.***

## 9 March

Tomorrow's Virgo supermoon will kick-start a fresh phase in your financial circumstances. This will occur due to developments at work, due to changes in your personal life or to particular news. If making agreements, check the fine print. ***Moon in Virgo.***

## 10 March

The Virgo supermoon will shine a light on your ability to be practical and reasonable when the chips are down. A romantic or idealistic outlook may turn your head, so be sensible now. You may hear significant news regarding money, travel or overseas. A significant legal matter or joint duty may be decided on. ***Moon enters Libra.***

## 11 March

Be positive and bold; you can make great progress. Some crabs will take the time for love and romance, while for others a trip, study course, project or legal matter could take a step in the right direction. ***Moon in Libra.***

## 12 March

The moon in Scorpio will connect you with your emotions and deeper senses such as your intuition, so trust your instincts. You'll appreciate the chance to get together with an old friend, or you may hear unexpectedly from someone from your past.

## 13 March

You'll enjoy that Friday feeling, even if it is Friday the 13th! You will feel inspired by art, beauty, music and your favourite people. Avoid seeing someone else's circumstances or weaknesses as a reflection of yours. You may bump into an old friend or hear from someone unexpectedly. ***Moon in Scorpio.***

## 14 March

You'll enjoy making the effort to do something different. If you are disappointed by someone's absence or by a change of plan, avoid allowing this to dampen your spirit. You will enjoy a fresh environment. Love can flourish, so take the initiative. Singles should mingle and couples find time to be together. ***Moon in Scorpio.***

## 15 March

This is a good day to make a commitment to someone you love, as your commitment is likely to blossom or may feel therapeutic to one or both partners. You may feel particularly inspired so art, writing and creativity will all flourish. ***Moon in Sagittarius.***

## 16 March

This is a good day to get ahead at work and with your many chores, but if obstacles seem to arise for you take things step by step and be methodical. ***Moon in Sagittarius.***

## 17 March

Today's Capricorn moon will help you to be practical and well organised, especially at work and with your various projects and ventures. You may feel inspired to meet someone on new terms. If you feel your insecurities rise, take practical steps to overcome them. ***Moon in Capricorn.***

## 18 March

You'll appreciate the opportunity to make plans and to collaborate and co-operate at work and with someone special. This is a good time to make a commitment to someone or to sign a contract, as long as you have done your research. Your projects can take steady and concrete steps forward. ***Moon in Capricorn.***

## 19 March

You will feel ready to make a commitment to someone special or to a plan of action. A lovely event could cement an agreement. Someone may commit to your plans, and you'll feel empowered as a result. Don't be afraid to step outside your comfort zone. ***Moon enters Aquarius.***

## 20 March

This is the equinox, when the sun enters Aries. You may receive important news from someone you share your life with or in relation to work or health. Developments may be swift, so ensure you are happy with the direction in which they are going or make plans to change your circumstances. ***Moon in Aquarius.***

## 21 March

The Pisces moon will add a romantic atmosphere to your weekend. You'll enjoy a visit somewhere new or quirky. You may meet an upbeat crowd who opens your eyes to fresher ways of looking at the bigger picture in life. You'll enjoy a reunion.

## 22 March

You'll enjoy an impromptu get together or unexpected developments and meetings. A partner or a friend may have a surprise for you. You'll enjoy being spontaneous and experiencing something new. ***Moon in Pisces.***

## 23 March

Today's events will kick-start a busy week. You'll feel inspired to follow your dreams, yet immediate concerns such as work, duties or a partner's circumstances will grab your attention. Be clear about your plans and remain true to yourself and your values. You could make great progress if you avoid feeling overly sensitive. ***Moon in Pisces.***

## 24 March

The Aries new moon suggests a therapeutic and upbeat development is possible with a project or person or at work. Take the initiative, and be ready to start something new when the opportunity arises. Avoid feeling vulnerable; look for the most therapeutic way forward. Someone may surprise you or you may be inclined to act without forethought, so think things through carefully.

## 25 March

As the sun aligns with Chiron you may find that your vulnerabilities or those of someone close may emerge. This is a good day to focus on a fresh perspective at work or towards someone special, and to opt for therapeutic activities or a health appointment. ***Moon in Aries.***

## 26 March

You may tend to have your heart on your sleeve or you may feel a little vulnerable. Show just what you're capable of and offer help if you're asked for it, especially at work or by someone with whom you must collaborate. Avoid arguments; you may need to show great strength or wisdom. ***Moon enters Taurus.***

## 27 March

You should find that romance and shared concerns become easier to handle over the upcoming weekend. Someone you work with or must rely on may behave unpredictably. If health has been a problem you'll gain traction and insight into the best way forward. ***Moon in Taurus.***

## 28 March

Love and romance could blossom. If you're working it will be a productive time. A trip will take you into fresh territory. You may meet a welcoming social group. ***Moon in Taurus.***

## 29 March

A change you have been looking forward to should be pleasant and could boost your personal life, such as your marriage or partnership. If you're working you should begin to see good results for all your efforts. ***Moon in Gemini.***

## 30 March

You can make binding agreements, so ensure you are happy with the plans you're putting in motion or make alternative arrangements. You'll enjoy the sense that your relationships and projects can all progress, but it may be an intense time of deep change so pace yourself. If you've felt stuck in life, be ready to move forward. ***Moon in Gemini.***

## 31 March

Events will gain their own momentum, so ensure you are happy with them. If not, consider how you might change your circumstances. Avoid feeling restless, and consult your intuition if you are unclear of where you stand. A clever plan, commitment or agreement can be made. ***Moon in Gemini.***

# APRIL

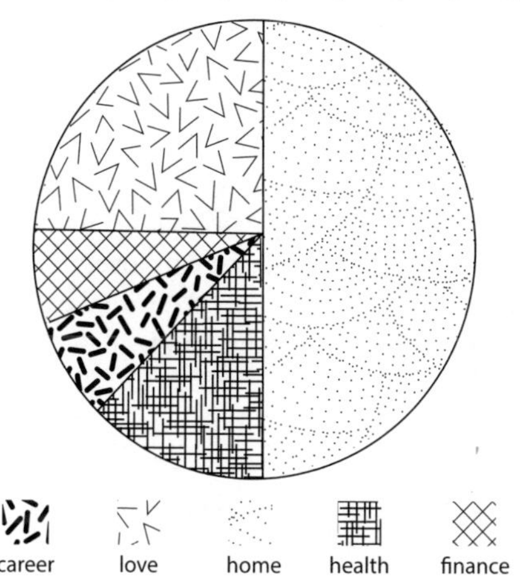


## 1 April

The moon in Cancer will motivate you to get in touch with old friends or colleagues and will put you in sync with your various projects and activities. Be true to yourself if arguments or complications arise; find ways to get around differences without arguments.

## 2 April

You'll appreciate the chance to give flight to some of your creativity, so don't be afraid to float your ideas for travel or fun projects and at work. ***Moon enters Leo.***

## 3 April

You'll appreciate the opportunity to indulge in a favourite past-time. A get together with someone you love will be enjoyable. This is a good day for meditation and spiritual work and for art, creativity and music. Avoid absent-mindedness. ***Moon in Leo.***

## 4 April

This is a good day to get ahead with your various chores and duties around the home. You'll appreciate the opportunity to meet someone you love; for romantics, love could certainly blossom. If you're working you should make progress. ***Moon in Leo.***

## 5 April

You may hear news from a partner or concerning money. Romance could be super intense. Areas you share in your life such as your home, work duties and finances will be the focus as some of these qualities are due considerable change. ***Moon in Virgo.***

## 6 April

Decisive news concerning a partner or work may have a strong impact on your day. You'll feel emotionally motivated to make changes in your life, and your motivation will propel you to succeed. Be creative and practical but avoid impulsiveness. ***Moon in Virgo.***

## 7 April

You are likely to hear unexpected news unless you did recently, in which case today's news will develop from there. This is a good day to discuss developments and to maintain a calm and helpful demeanour. Communications could either go very well or not very well. Look for balance and you could scale mountains. ***Moon in Libra.***

## 8 April

Today's supermoon in Libra will shine a light on how you can find balance in your personal life. It may revolve around your home and family or around how to deal with key developments that affect relationships. Talks and negotiations will help you to find the balance.

## 9 April

Today's Scorpio moon will get you in touch with your feelings. Trust your intuition and aim to work towards solutions to any issues that arise. ***Moon in Scorpio.***

## 10 April

You may be surprised by news to do with work or the past. This could be a healing time, but if events bring your vulnerabilities to the surface aim to connect with those you know support you and who matter the most to you. ***Moon in Scorpio.***

## 11 April

There is a therapeutic quality to the weekend, especially in connection with someone whose company you love or work with. It's a good day for health and beauty treats and to focus on building solid relationships with those you love. ***Moon enters Sagittarius.***

## 12 April

This is a good day to talk and for organising shared ventures. A social get together should be enjoyable, and if you're working you will make good progress. A commitment may be made, so if you'd like to take your relationship to the next level it's a good time to find out if your partner is on board. ***Moon in Sagittarius.***

## 13 April

This is an excellent phase for you to be venturing ahead at work and with your various partnerships and relationships. Just remember you cannot agree with everyone all the time! Take things step by step and aim to make solid agreements with those with whom you must collaborate. Someone you love may surprise you. ***Moon enters Capricorn.***

## 14 April

You may be surprised by developments. If you tend to rise to challenges you'll succeed, both at work and in your ventures and personal life, but you must avoids conflict as it will get you nowhere fast. A get together may be spontaneous or impromptu. ***Moon in Capricorn.***

## 15 April

Ensure you are tactful and mindful of other people's feelings. You may feel extra sensitive yourself, so be strong and open minded and discuss your circumstances with people with whom you collaborate. A trip somewhere healing such as into nature will please you. ***Moon enters Aquarius.***

## 16 April

Today's moon in Aquarius will open up the door to new options and end a stalemate if discussions have been difficult. Think outside the square and be ready to be the bigger person to avoid escalating a difference of opinion into conflict. A favourite activity will feel refreshing.

## 17 April

Be inspired! Take some time out to consider your circumstances purely from a positive point of view. Be optimistic; you have some wonderful friends and supporters. Aim to make the changes you know must be made even if they seem daunting. ***Moon enters Pisces.***

## 18 April

You'll enjoy a sociable or busy weekend. This is an excellent day for get togethers and talks, and a trip could be fruitful. It's also a good time for talking, so if you have a bridge to mend consider mending it today. Romance can blossom, so arrange a treat. ***Moon in Pisces***.

## 19 April

You may feel spontaneous and motivated to be more outgoing or to try something new. It's a good day to discuss joint duties and responsibilities such as finances, as you're likely to reach mutually acceptable conclusions. Romance could flourish. ***Moon in Pisces.***

## 20 April

As the sun enters Taurus you will feel more practical about making changes at work or in a relationship as the weeks go by; you may already sense this is possible. You can make great progress with careful attention to detail while maintaining a fresh perspective. You may be surprised by news. ***Moon enters Aries.***

## 21 April

If you react well to pressure you could excel, particularly with someone special or a group, friend or colleague. You may need to rise to a challenge or overcome a difference of opinion. If you are super sensitive, aim to boost your self-confidence with positive self-talk. An authority figure may have news for you. ***Moon in Aries.***

## 22 April

This is a good day to talk, as those you communicate with may be sympathetic to your ideas and views. You may enjoy an uplifting experience such as a trip somewhere beautiful or the chance to indulge in romance, art and music. Avoid forgetfulness. ***Moon in Aries.***

## 23 April

Today's Taurus new moon represents a fresh interest for you; you may be attracted to a new social circle or friendship. For some mid-July crabs a fresh cycle is about to begin in your career, general direction or status. Be practical with your decisions, but avoid restricting your options too much.

## 24 April

Today's moon in Taurus will encourage you to indulge in life's delights; you may wish to organise events that are truly epicurean and indulge in your favourite past-times in your spare time. It is Friday, after all! This is a good day to be practical, reasonable and methodical with developments, so complete chores before you dive into delights.

## 25 April

The Gemini moon and Mercury square Pluto suggest potential disagreements, so take things step by step. If you're feeling restless, take breaks and consult your friends or partner and those who rely on you to ensure you're all on the same page.

There's no reason you can't see eye to eye, but you may need to make concessions.

## 26 April

Expect a surprise or a change of atmosphere or place. You may hear unexpectedly from a friend or will enjoy an impromptu get together. Events could signal the start of something completely new or different. Communications may be strained, so be clear and willing to compromise. ***Moon in Gemini.***

## 27 April

When you feel things are up in the air it's important not to pre-empt an outcome, as you can rush the process and pressure people into answers they're not ready to give. Avoid speaking out of turn as you may regret impulsiveness. Communications should begin to settle soon. Be brave, but avoid conflict. ***Moon in Gemini.***

## 28 April

Mercury in Taurus will enable communications to slow down and for action to be taken after much discussion. Some communications may be stuck or delayed, so be patient. If you're travelling, plan ahead to avoid delays. ***Moon enters Cancer.***

## 29 April

A partner, work colleague or authority figure may have news, and a project may take a turn in a different direction. If you have already made a decision, review it to ensure you're happy before you go too far down a particular road. Avoid letting people down unnecessarily or taking their weaknesses personally. ***Moon in Cancer.***

## 30 April

You'll feel more outspoken about your feelings concerning developments and motivated to mend bridges and move forward with a positive attitude. Avoid stirring up old resentments. You may be surprised by the information or news you receive. ***Moon enters Leo.***

# MAY

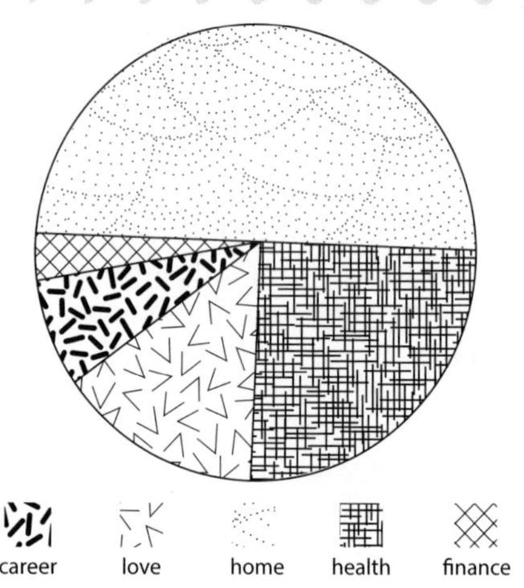


## 1 May

A friend, group or organisation may surprise you with their news, or you may receive unexpected news. A trip somewhere different or exciting could be just what you want to breathe fresh air into your routine. Avoid speaking out of turn at work; you may regret it. ***Moon in Leo.***

## 2 May

The earthy Virgo moon this weekend will help you enjoy a relaxed time, even if you do something different for a change. A shopping spree or the chance to invest a little time in yourself will certainly appeal and should prove enjoyable. Leave the credit card at home if you're already in debt.

## 3 May

The strong earthy feel to the weekend will prove to be stabilising for you. You'll enjoy meeting with dependable people you know well and finding support and nurturance from them. ***Moon in Virgo.***

## 4 May

You may be inclined to have your head in the clouds a little, so take your time to get on board at work. Romance could blossom and you'll feel creative, but you must be careful to avoid forgetfulness and avoid allowing your imagination run away with you. ***Moon enters Libra.***

## 5 May

Key news or developments will be ideal for getting down to basics with arrangements with a friend or at work or regarding your long-term status and activities. Key personal, work or health matters may be determined. Avoid fuzzy thinking. ***Moon in Libra.***

## 6 May

This is a good day to get things done, for paperwork, domestic matters and collaborating with groups, friends and partners or your favourite projects. In the lead up to tomorrow's Scorpio full moon some people or events may seem more intense than usual. If so, take things step by step. ***Moon enters Scorpio.***

## 7 May

Today's Scorpio full moon signals the start of a new phase in your domestic life or concerning family, a relationship or property. For some mid-July crabs there will be a new chapter regarding an agreement to do with work or your status. A new device may make communications easier.

## 8 May

This is a good day to talk and to discuss your various plans, both at work and in your personal life. It's also a good day to indulge in romance, art and music. ***Moon enters Sagittarius.***

## 9 May

You'll enjoy catching up with someone you admire and whose company you enjoy. A trip will be enjoyable. Working crabs will be super productive, and a meeting or news could signal changes to come at work. ***Moon in Sagittarius.***

## 10 May

There are ideal aspects to your day. News or a get together will bring you closer to someone who has a powerful influence in your life. You'll enjoy a social event. A change of routine should be enjoyable. ***Moon enters Capricorn.***

## 11 May

There will be a free flow of information so it's a good day to talk, but communications may involve misunderstandings and travel may be delayed so be patient with developments. Communications will improve tomorrow if not before. Avoid rushing and pushing for results. Back up computers to avoid losing information. ***Moon in Aquarius.***

## 12 May

Now that Mercury is in Gemini you should begin to see communications and travel-related matters get back on track. A particular agreement or duty may take your focus and will need attention. You will enjoy a get together with a friend or a business meeting. Romance could blossom. ***Moon enters Aquarius.***

## 13 May

As Mars enters dreamy Pisces you may find that some communications are a little delayed or vague, so be patient. You will feel more creative and inspired at work and with your various projects. The next six weeks is a good phase for self-development. ***Moon in Aquarius.***

## 14 May

As Venus begins a retrograde phase an agreement or matter of principle may take your focus. This may be to do with love, work, friendship, health or money. Avoid fuzzy thinking; be careful about your decisions now. Consider how love and money reflect your energy levels, and aim to boost your energy. ***Moon in Aquarius.***

## 15 May

As Jupiter turns retrograde the pressure in an agreement or a relationship will begin to ease, although matters may first reach a turning point. You should be able to come to an agreement over an area you share such as work. ***Moon in Pisces.***

## 16 May

This is a good day to make a commitment to a person or a plan, and to make agreements with someone you share space or duties with. If you have argued you can reach a compromise. Avoid being hasty; take your time to ensure your decisions are what you want long term. ***Moon in Pisces.***

## 17 May

This is a good day for a trip, get togethers and discussions, and for meetings and romance. If you're working it is likely to be a busy or a lucrative day. You may even experience a lucky break. ***Moon in Pisces.***

## 18 May

The Aries moon will help to motivate you, especially at work and with your shared ventures. You may feel a little vulnerable, so take things step by step. If you need help don't be afraid to ask for it or to delegate work. Someone may ask you for help.

## 19 May

You have get up and go but not everyone will agree with you, despite key ventures powering ahead. There may be some aspects of confusion that come from a lack of shared knowledge or experience, so be clear in your interactions to avoid conundrums and be bold. ***Moon in Aries.***

## 20 May

If you thrive on a little tension either at work or in your love life then success is yours, but if you prefer things to be plain sailing you will need to avoid being frustrated by delays and conundrums. Avoid impatience and be positive. ***Moon in Taurus.***

## 21 May

Now that the sun is in Gemini you'll enjoy the sense that communications and relationships will improve, but you must avoid making assumptions. Be super clear with discussions and diligent and hard-working and you will reap the rewards. ***Moon in Taurus.***

## 22 May

Tomorrow's Gemini new moon will kick-start a fresh phase in your career or status. It will mean a fresh daily routine or the chance to boost health. A friendship, partnership or connection with a group or organisation could signal a new contract or commitment; be clear about the terms.

## 23 May

With the new moon and the sun, Venus and Mercury all in chatty Gemini it is likely to be a busy day; for some there will be key trips and agreements to attend to. A new understanding or development to do with work or someone close dictates you must be clear, or mistakes can be made. Avoid misunderstandings and delays.

## 24 May

If misunderstandings or a lack of knowledge have been evident over the past few days, you can go a long way to make up for this today. A meeting, news or a development should be positive or even therapeutic. Stick with your plans and be optimistic. ***Moon in Gemini.***

## 25 May

You'll appreciate a change of pace and you may be surprised by news or an impromptu get together. You may bump into an old friend or hear unexpected news from a partner. ***Moon enters Cancer.***

## 26 May

Today's moon in Cancer will feel settling as you will gain insight into someone close or with whom you work. You will also feel more equipped to deal with changes or moving goal posts. This is a good day to clear the air with anyone with whom you have had recent disagreements.

## 27 May

Be careful with communications as mistakes can be made. If you're travelling, plan ahead to avoid delays. Back up computers and be patient with communications at work. If you're tired, rest up. ***Moon in Cancer.***

## 28 May

As communications magnet Mercury prepares to enter your sign, key information may come to light. You may enjoy hearing from an old friend or travelling to an old haunt. Avoid snap decisions and rely on your gut feelings. ***Moon in Leo.***

## 29 May

With Mercury in your sign you should become more instinctive, and you'll feel you can trust your intuition more over the next few weeks. There is a therapeutic aspect to the day. You may enjoy a healthy treat. Surprise news or an impromptu get together should be enjoyable. ***Moon enters Virgo.***

## 30 May

Today's earthy Virgo moon will help you to get your feet on the ground with your various plans and ventures. You'll enjoy doing something different, and a fresh environment or group of people will be enjoyable. Avoid arguments; aim to find out more factual information if conflict is brewing.

## 31 May

A visit to someone's house or the arrival of a guest will be enjoyable. This is an excellent day to catch up with friends and indulge in your favourite activities. You'll enjoy socialising, music, art, film, writing, reading and dancing along with resting and recuperating. ***Moon enters Libra.***

# JUNE

## 1 June

Adopt a balanced approach to events and you'll get ahead in dynamic ways. Trust that your past decisions have been correct, but be prepared to adjust to present circumstances. ***Moon in Libra.***

## 2 June

You are communicating well, so avoid being thrown off course by the lack of clarity exhibited by others. Aim to work together creatively and imaginatively with them. Be clear in your communications and events will fall in place. ***Moon in Libra.***

## 3 June

You cannot agree with everyone all the time; news and developments may be decisive even if you do not agree with them. If news is unclear aim to find the facts you need. Avoid impatience, and try to enjoy your day without arguments. ***Moon in Scorpio.***

## 4 June

Developments will gain a momentum of their own, and yet you may wish to stop them. Consider your true values and priorities and be clear and open to new ideas. An impromptu get together, health or work development should boost your optimism. ***Moon enters Sagittarius.***

## 5 June

Tomorrow's partial lunar eclipse in Sagittarius may bring an unexpected change your way, to do with work or your personal life. You may feel more creative and outgoing than usual, and an adventurous idea is likely to appeal to you. Avoid arguments.

## 6 June

The eclipse may spotlight a difference of opinion, challenge or development that will require you to be super focused and motivated. Be practical and patient; avoid locking horns with someone you must get on with such as a teacher, health professional or employer. Gather information so you can take action from an informed stance. ***Moon enters Capricorn.***

## 7 June

The Capricorn moon will encourage you to be practical about your various projects, especially at work. Strengthen your mindset, particularly if you feel some truths need to be spoken or that you are in a vulnerable position. ***Moon in Capricorn.***

## 8 June

You may receive good news from the past. If health has been an issue you should gain insight into the best way forward. This is a good day for a health or beauty appointment. You may enjoy a reunion. ***Moon in Capricorn.***

## 9 June

Consider thinking outside the square, as you will gain insight into the best way forward with a business or personal partner. You'll enjoy doing something new. ***Moon enters Aquarius.***

## 10 June

You'll enjoy socialising and networking. Avoid people who give you mixed messages and aim to be inspired by art, romance, music and reading. ***Moon in Aquarius.***

## 11 June

An impromptu event should be enjoyable, so be spontaneous. A confusing or unusual event needn't get the better of you. Aim to work with developments that seem out of the ordinary,

and ask for support from resources that you wouldn't usually use. ***Moon enters Pisces.***

## 12 June

Today's moon in Pisces will help you get in touch with your feelings, and you should enjoy getting closer to someone you love. Aim for mutually enjoyable past-times; you'll be glad you did! Try to get to the bottom of mixed messages. ***Moon in Pisces.***

## 13 June

If you love romance and mystery – and which Cancerian doesn't love romance? – you'll enjoy both. Organise an event if you haven't already. Spiritual crabs will enjoy meditation and visualisation. The arts and music will appeal, but you may need to focus extra hard if you're working. Avoid feeling frustrated by delays and absent-mindedness. ***Moon enters Aries.***

## 14 June

You're better known for being sensitive and gentle, yet your soft inner self is encased in a hard shell. You can be tough, and today's moon in Aries will bring your inner strength out. You may surprise yourself with your ability to bounce back from disappointment and overcome vulnerabilities. You may be asked for help. ***Moon in Aries.***

## 15 June

Some relationships and communications may become a little more intense than you'd imagined, so maintain perspective to avoid feeling disheartened by someone else's mood or news. A health matter is best approached with a view to self-improvement. ***Moon in Aries***.

## 16 June

A question of what is right and what is wrong may be at the basis of some conversations or issues. Try to establish common ground with someone special or with a work matter to avoid disputes. Be practical with long-term change. ***Moon enters Taurus.***

## 17 June

The improvements you wish to see at work, in your personal life or regarding a shared duty will begin to manifest. It's important to avoid arguments, as these could become explosive. Find ways to establish common ground and agreement instead. ***Moon in Taurus.***

## 18 June

Be prepared to go the extra mile at work or with someone special, as your efforts are likely to pay off. Events may gather momentum, so ensure you are happy with the way they are rolling or make plans to change your circumstances. ***Moon enters Gemini.***

## 19 June

Take your time to consider someone else's opinions, as this could work in your favour. Avoid feeling you must agree with everyone, but take the time to see the merit in a collaboration or fresh interest. This may be a busy day. ***Moon in Gemini.***

## 20 June

Prepare for a busy weekend; you may be surprised by news from a partner or someone close. A visit, trip or favourite activity should be upbeat. You may feel optimistic and will enjoy socialising. ***Moon in Gemini.***

## 21 June

Now that the sun is in Cancer you'll appreciate improved energy levels over the next four weeks. Today's ring of fire solar eclipse points to a new phase in your personal life, especially if it's your birthday. For many Cancerians the solar eclipse marks a fresh chapter at work or in health and daily routines. ***Moon in Cancer.***

## 22 June

This is a good day to take the time to review how you feel about circumstances. Change is inevitable, so carefully plan how to move forward through your projects and circumstances. A partnership or work may require special attention. ***Moon in Cancer.***

## 23 June

Trust your instincts, especially in connection with big picture goals such as your career and interests, relationships and experiences. You should begin to feel a little less introspective and more outgoing over the next two days, so plan for some upbeat events during the week. ***Moon enters Leo.***

## 24 June

The Leo moon will motivate you to be upbeat, especially about your various projects and at work. Shared areas of your life will merit careful focus, and you'll be ready to address any vulnerabilities by taking direct action. ***Moon in Leo***.

## 25 June

A Venus ends its retrograde phase you should begin to see your ideas and relationships move forward over the news few weeks and months. There may be particular work, financial or personal matters to attend to to ensure you can move ahead well. Be ready to reassess your values if necessary. ***Moon enters Virgo.***

## 26 June

This is a good day to consider how you can move forward with a group, friend or organisation, and to talk with people about matters that have been on your mind in practical ways and with a view to establishing a reasonable outcome. ***Moon in Virgo.***

## 27 June

This is a good day to be practical with paperwork, communications and financial matters. Tie up loose ends in any of these areas and plan ahead for holidays, time out and work schedules. A lovely social event should be enjoyable. ***Moon enters Libra.***

## 28 June

As Mars enters Aries, where it will be for the rest of the year, you should feel clearer about many of your aims and interests, especially those to do with work and shared responsibilities and finances. Information or events may already point you in a dynamic direction that could put clever plans to work. ***Moon in Libra.***

## 29 June

Today's Libra moon will put you in the mood to sort out any areas that seem unbalanced or unjust. You must avoid appearing overtly bossy, aggressive or eccentric. You may be surprised by good news from your past regarding health or work.

## 30 June

Someone close may express intense feelings or give you the heads-up about their true feelings. You'll enjoy a reunion or the chance to clear up a past matter. Developments may take you back to matters you were deciding on early in April. ***Moon enters Scorpio.***

# JULY

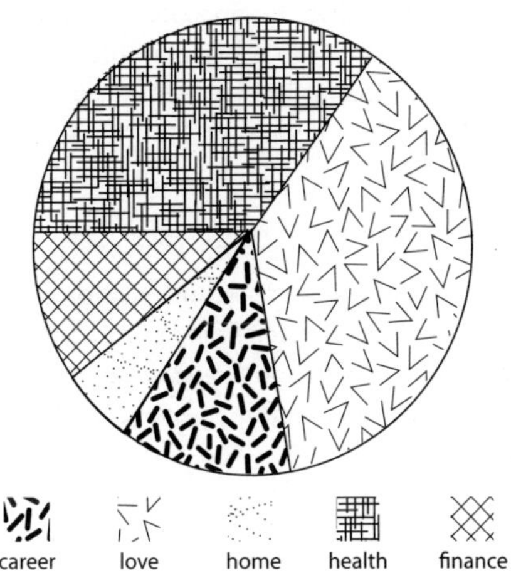


## 1 July

This is a good day for a health appointment. News from your past or a reunion or get together may be more significant than meets the eye. You may be surprised by events or bump into an old friend; avoid taking developments personally. Be prepared to work hard to improve your circumstances. ***Moon in Scorpio.***

## 2 July

Times can be intense and stressful between two eclipses, so relax if you're experiencing the pressure. You should be feeling more positive. Keep an eye on misunderstandings and mistakes. If you're assimilating recent developments, take time out. ***Moon enters Sagittarius.***

## 3 July

You are a water sign so you're intuitive, though you may be inclined to ignore your instincts. Take a moment to tune in to your heart and follow your inner guidance. You'll enjoy being active and outgoing, so organise an event or a treat. ***Moon in Sagittarius.***

## 4 July

With Venus in Gemini you'll be feeling sociable. Today's Capricorn moon will encourage you to be practical, especially at work and with your various duties. Find the balance and you'll enjoy the best of both worlds. ***Moon enters Capricorn.***

## 5 July

The partial lunar eclipse in Capricorn signifies a fresh phase in a business or personal partnership, especially if you were born on or before 7 July. If you were born afterwards you'll see a fresh chapter at work or in your health or daily life. Plan ahead and strategise to make solid agreements that will last in these key areas.

## 6 July

You will make progress by being practical, reasonable and measured. If you try to push things along that you know can only progress at their own pace you may be disappointed. Be inspired but also be realistic. ***Moon enters Aquarius.***

## 7 July

Today's moon in Aquarius may bring your quirky, independent side out and you may feel a little rebellious. Aim to enjoy downtime with like-minded friends, but you may need to buckle down at work first. ***Moon in Aquarius.***

## 8 July

You may feel restless and inclined to act rashly. If communications are rushed or stuck, take your time and be patient with people less bright than you, especially at work and regarding health and well-being. ***Moon in Aquarius.***

## 9 July

You'll appreciate the opportunity to let your imagination loose and be creative and inspired. You may gain insight into someone special and share romantic times. You may also be prone to daydreaming, so avoid making important decisions unless you have all the facts. ***Moon in Pisces.***

## 10 July

As the moon joins Neptune in Pisces you'll feel closer to those you love and will enjoy getting together over mutual interests such as art, creativity, music, film and dance. You may also tend to be escapist and will enjoy travel. Avoid overindulgence if you decide to socialise. Romance could blossom. ***Moon in Pisces***.

## 11 July

There is an upbeat feeling to the weekend and you'll enjoy giving full rein to your active side, enjoying walks, sport or the chance to do something different. ***Moon enters Aries***.

## 12 July

You'll enjoy being spontaneous but must avoid impulsiveness, or you may regret having spoken out of turn or making rash decisions. You may enjoy a surprise. You'll appreciate doing something active and bold that enriches the senses, such as a visit to the ocean. ***Moon in Aries.***

## 13 July

This could be an action-packed day; you may be motivated to excel in a favourite activity or at work. You may be inclined to overwork, act rashly or overestimate your potential, so be measured and careful. Avoid erratic drivers and speaking without forethought. You may be asked for help. ***Moon enters Taurus***.

## 14 July

An important financial or work decision is on the cards. If it's your birthday, an important or intense event will be a feature in your day. Be inspired and avoid making purely emotional decisions. This could be a romantic time when considerable commitments are made. If you argue with someone aim to find a solution. ***Moon in Taurus.***

## 15 July

You'll gain deeper insight into circumstances, especially to do with a business or personal partner. Emotions may be deep or intense. You can make changes that could be long standing. A friend or organisation may be helpful. You'll enjoy socialising or doing something different, especially if it's your birthday. ***Moon in Taurus.***

## 16 July

You'll enjoy being spontaneous. A surprise or the chance to do something different either at work or in your spare time will be enjoyable. Don't be afraid to embrace change. ***Moon enters Gemini.***

## 17 July

The moon in Gemini will encourage you to be chatty and sociable and try something new. If work duties must be completed and subsequently you're super tired, this is a fantastic evening to put your feet up and cocoon.

## 18 July

Key decisions merit care and attention. Take your time this weekend to ensure you're on the right track, both in your personal life and health-wise. If you feel you must make some alterations here and there take your time doing so and be ready to be flexible in the process of change. ***Moon enters Cancer.***

## 19 July

You'll enjoy the moon in Cancer as you'll feel at home and inspired in your endeavours. Even if you feel you must keep some of your thoughts to yourself you'll appreciate the opportunity to enjoy the company of like-minded people. ***Moon in Cancer.***

## 20 July

Tomorrow's Cancerian new moon represents the chance to revitalise your personal life and appearance and, for some, your daily routine and health. A particular partnership may be on your mind, and the new moon will encourage you to make the changes you'd ideally like to see. Be inspired but also realistic.

## 21 July

The new moon will spotlight certain relationships that could be more positive or supportive, especially those at work or in your personal life. You may be asked for help. Avoid misunderstandings by being super clear. A health matter may need to be reviewed. Avoid erratic drivers. ***Moon enters Leo.***

## 22 July

You may hear unexpected good news or from someone from your past from out of the blue. If you're waiting for the green light it is likely to arrive. Someone may prove to be super helpful. ***Moon in Leo.***

## 23 July

Be realistic and establish clear boundaries about how you wish to proceed with a shared area such as finances and at work. Ask yourself what and who your priorities are. Someone you have a strong connection with may have other priorities, but if they are supportive you should find common ground. ***Moon enters Virgo.***

## 24 July

Follow your dreams but be practical and realistic along the way. You have the chance to boost your circumstances in practical ways; just ensure your communications and actions all lead to your wonderful goals. Avoid feeling distracted and being reckless and pushing for results. ***Moon in Virgo.***

## 25 July

You'll appreciate the opportunity to get together with people you love. You may also need to fulfil certain duties, be these at work or chores around the house or with particular family members. ***Moon in Libra.***

## 26 July

Communications maestro Mercury is in your sign and is bringing your inner chatterbox out, although you may not always agree with everyone so be choosy about who you spend your time with. A trip somewhere lovely or a get together will raise morale. Romance could blossom. ***Moon in Libra.***

## 27 July

You may be tempted to speak before you think which could add pressure, so do your research before you wade into debates and avoid speaking out of turn. You'll enjoy a trip or favourite activity or the chance to touch base with a colleague or someone you admire. Romance could blossom. ***Moon enters Scorpio.***

## 28 July

Your inner feelings will come out and you'll appreciate having a friend or family member who is a good sounding board or shoulder to lean on. Romance, art, music and dance will appeal. If making decisions, ensure you have all the facts. ***Moon in Scorpio.***

## 29 July

Good communication skills are the key to your success. Focus on making things work better, both for yourself and those you live and work with; you'll enjoy positive results. ***Moon enters Sagittarius.***

## 30 July

Key news will arrive, especially if you were born on 11 or 12 July. All crabs will receive important news or may have a key decision to make. A get together, trip or event may be reason to celebrate. ***Moon enters Sagittarius.***

## 31 July

You should hear good news, but if the opposite happens there will be an option to improve circumstance and for healing and a positive outcome. ***Moon enters Capricorn.***

# AUGUST

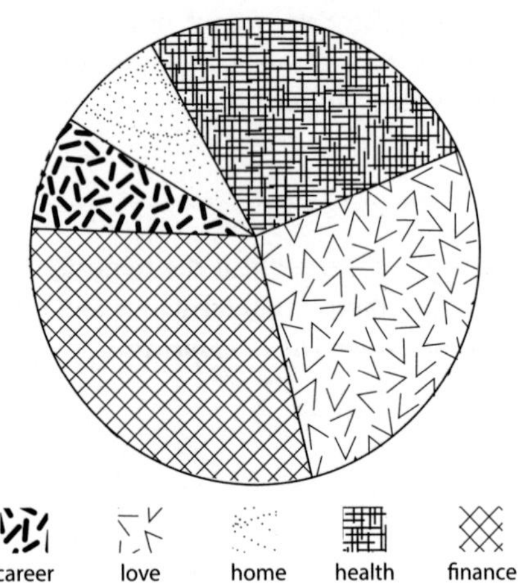


## 1 August

Serious or intense interactions this weekend will put a relationship, work or health matter in a clearer light. Whether you find events tough or empowering, it is an excellent weekend to get down to the nitty gritty of your decisions or a relationship. ***Moon in Capricorn.***

## 2 August

You may be surprised by some conversations or financial transactions; be ready to think on your feet. Luckily, someone from your past or at work will prove helpful. ***Moon enters Aquarius***.

## 3 August

Tomorrow's Aquarian full moon will spotlight a business or personal partnership. You may find interesting ways to brighten up an existing arrangement or will agree on new terms. A joint financial or personal arrangement may benefit from a fresh agreement. Singles may meet a quirky character.

## 4 August

The full moon shines a light on your agreements and arrangements and it will be in your interest to look for ways to compromise, especially if disagreements are brewing. You may find some interactions difficult, but you should manage to establish a good outcome. ***Moon in Aquarius.***

## 5 August

As Mercury enters Leo communications will be more upbeat over the next two weeks; for some lucky crabs, finances may improve. You may risk being super generous or throwing caution to the wind, so be prudent over the next two weeks. ***Moon enters Pisces.***

## 6 August

Interactions should be better and you may enjoy immersing yourself in a motivational project or interest. Romance could blossom, so organise an event or an evening in. Avoid forgetfulness and vagueness; do your research if making big decisions. ***Moon in Pisces.***

## 7 August

As Venus enters your sign your attention will focus on love and money over the next month, and you may find that some events already place your attention there. The Aries moon will encourage you to be outgoing and bold.

## 8 August

You'll enjoy an upbeat, active or sporty weekend and may be ready for a therapeutic or life-enhancing venture. Nature, the outdoors and generally being active will appeal to you. ***Moon in Aries.***

## 9 August

You prefer to go with the flow yet sometimes in life there are new opportunities or changes that will simply ask you to be decisive and act on your intuition. This is such a time! Be ready to try something new; take the initiative, but avoid impulsiveness or rash decisions. ***Moon in Aries***.

## 10 August

Unexpected news or a change of schedule needn't get in the way of an otherwise productive and progressive day. A financial matter may need careful handling. If you're travelling, plan ahead to avoid delays. Back up computers and be careful with communications to avoid misunderstandings. ***Moon in Taurus.***

## 11 August

Take the time to get to the bottom of a financial, work or personal matter. Avoid allowing problems to fester. Be positive and practical at work; you have the ability to overcome any hurdles that present. Back up computers. ***Moon in Taurus.***

## 12 August

The details will be important: at work, financially or in your personal life regarding shared assets and duties. If you are unclear about details, research your options. An inspiring idea or activity is worth pursuing. ***Moon enters Gemini.***

## 13 August

Mars at the zenith of your chart is pushing you forward to be a dynamic achiever. In this position you can encounter opposition, and today is one such day. Avoid ego or power struggles. Find constructive ways to be strong while not getting caught in the drama. ***Moon in Gemini.***

## 14 August

Be careful with communications and financial transactions. If you're travelling, double check itineraries and leave plenty of time for delays. If information you receive or talks you have are unclear, find out more. ***Moon in Gemini.***

## 15 August

You show great potential, and the areas in your life that you wish to change will demand you be strong or assert yourself. Avoid being daunted by tasks. Exert yourself and you could excel. ***Moon enters Cancer.***

## 16 August

You should see great results for all your hard work; you may even appreciate a fresh opportunity that comes your way at work, financially or regarding a favourite interest. A lovely get together will be upbeat and enjoyable. This is still a volatile time, so you must ensure you avoid arguments as they could spiral. ***Moon in Cancer.***

## 17 August

Key news, a specific financial transaction or a trip somewhere lovely will be a focal point of your day. News may be decisive. You may feel emotional about some aspects of developments, so avoid impulsive actions. ***Moon enters Leo.***

## 18 August

Key discussions may be more complex than you'd hoped. Someone in a position of authority may have news for you. Key financial transactions are best handled very carefully and with the full details at your fingertips. A debt may be repaid. You may find you hear unexpectedly from someone from your past. ***Moon in Leo.***

## 19 August

Today's Leo new moon suggests news will open doors for you. You're ready for an exciting new adventure, which could mean travel, a new digital device, a fresh relationship if you're single or a different way to save money so you can spend more on exciting ventures.

## 20 August

You'll appreciate the sense that you can get to the nitty gritty of some of your ideas and ventures so that your plans can begin to take shape. For many crabs this is a rewarding if busy time. ***Moon in Virgo.***

## 21 August

Conversations and interactions with work colleagues and those you share other aspects of your life with should improve. If you have plans you must schedule it's a good day for get togethers to work on long-term plans. Avoid snap decisions; take things step by step. ***Moon enters Libra.***

## 22 August

You'll appreciate the opportunity to spend some time improving your home and focusing on those you love the most. You'll enjoy improving your décor and working on bringing harmony into your home or family. ***Moon in Libra.***

## 23 August

If you feel like meeting up with old friends or family this could be a wonderful time spent with those you love. You may need to compromise about which activities you'll do as your plans may differ from those of everyone else. ***Moon in Scorpio.***

## 24 August

If you tend to rise to a challenge you'll enjoy today's dynamics, as you could excel with work and collaborative ventures. If you dislike tension you may need to take extra breaks and pace yourself. Avoid obstinacy and making rash decisions. ***Moon in Scorpio.***

## 25 August

This is a good day for a breakthrough, so aim to take the initiative where your plans have been difficult to implement or where communications have been stuck. You may hear unexpected news or bump into an old friend. If you have a decision to make, ensure you have all the facts. Avoid arguments. ***Moon enters Sagittarius.***

## 26 August

A financial, personal or work matter can progress. You can get a great deal done and may appreciate a therapeutic aspect to your day. This is a good time for romance, but you must focus on the details at work as you may be absent-minded. ***Moon in Sagittarius.***

## 27 August

There is a romantic atmosphere; you'll enjoy celebrating all that life has to offer and indulging in your favourite activities. You may enjoy a trip somewhere beautiful to hear music or watch a movie. You may receive a financial or an ego boost. Spiritual crabs will gain insight via meditation and prayer. ***Moon enters Capricorn.***

## 28 August

The moon in Capricorn will promote solid and steady progress for you, especially at work and with your various interests. Avoid getting stuck in a rut; think laterally. A trip, visit or favourite interest could be inspiring, so organise something special. ***Moon in Capricorn.***

## 29 August

You may enjoy a boost in self-esteem this weekend. You'll appreciate a health or beauty treat. You'll enjoy travelling somewhere beautiful or a change of routine. This is a good weekend to talk, especially if you're reconsidering a decision. ***Moon in Capricorn.***

## 30 August

Romance could blossom and feelings may be intense, so remain level headed if you feel emotional or caught in a drama. Avoid allowing someone's intense feelings to overly influence you. Check the details if you're making important decisions or travelling, as there may be some facts that are missing. Avoid absent-mindedness. ***Moon enters Aquarius.***

## 31 August

Key communications and transactions may be liable to be a little confused or even complex so be patient, especially at work and regarding someone's feelings. A trip may be delayed or you will need to double check your itinerary. This is a good day for a health or medical appointment. ***Moon in Aquarius.***

# SEPTEMBER

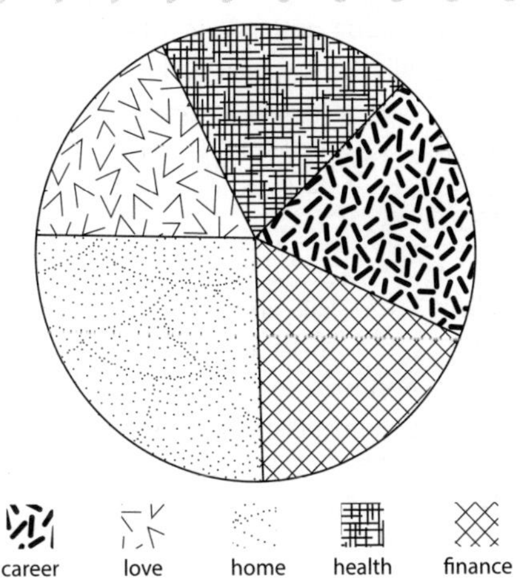


## 1 September

This is a good day for communications, as long as you maintain perspective and avoid allowing someone to run away with the context and take over the discussion. Some crabs will enjoy a lovely trip or get together. ***Moon enters Pisces.***

## 2 September

Today's full moon in Pisces will be inspiring. For some crabs there will be a beguiling and magical feeling to the day; for others, romance will ignite passion. This is a good time to consider how you wish a special project, trip or relationship to progress. Be realistic as well as enchanted!

## 3 September

This is an excellent day for talks and for getting down to basics with your various plans, and to make agreements regarding your long-term arrangements. You may be ready to make a commitment to someone special or to a financial matter. ***Moon enters Aries.***

## 4 September

This is an ideal day for bringing more beauty, love and joy into your home and life in general. You'll enjoy a lovely get together that will remind you how important it is to connect with like-minded and supportive people. Romance may blossom, but if you experience an argument it may come down to a difference in values. ***Moon in Aries.***

## 5 September

You're more known for your gentleness and sensitivity, yet you can be very strong and outgoing. This weekend you'll enjoy doing something exciting, upbeat and active. A trip that takes you somewhere new could be revitalising. Avoid taking the random comments of others personally. ***Moon in Aries.***

## 6 September

Where there have been arguments, difficult communications, tension or drama you will appreciate the opportunity to relax and attract more harmony and balance in your life in practical ways, such as bringing flowers into your house or playing calming music. ***Moon in Taurus.***

## 7 September

There is much to be excited about in your life, and the more practical and methodical you are the better for you. If you experience some residual tension with someone, aim to charm and enjoy inspiring activities. ***Moon in Taurus.***

## 8 September

You'll appreciate the opportunity to get down to the nitty gritty with someone you must collaborate with in your daily life; you should gain a sense of empowerment when you do. Aim to organise a lovely event for today or tomorrow; you should enjoy something fun. ***Moon enters Gemini.***

## 9 September

A lovely change to your usual routine such as a get together or trip should feel empowering or at least pleasant. Upbeat news is on the way. For some lucky crabs today's developments will revolve around love and money; these should be positive. ***Moon in Gemini.***

## 10 September

Conversations and travel may take you somewhere interesting, but you must be careful to avoid delays and misunderstandings. This is a good day to obtain advice from an expert. If you're travelling, plan ahead and check your itinerary. Avoid erratic drivers. Back up computers to avoid losing information. ***Moon in Gemini.***

## 11 September

Romance will appeal; you may experience a lovely event that includes music, dance, good food and drink or visit a beautiful place that inspires you. Spiritual crabs should gain deep insight. This is an excellent day for art, creativity and writing. Avoid forgetfulness, and be careful to check financial and contractual details. ***Moon enters Cancer.***

## 12 September

You may be surprised by news or a visit and may need to change your plans at a moment's notice. Your efforts will be worthwhile even if logistics are complex, so remain optimistic and look for the best-case outcome. ***Moon in Cancer.***

## 13 September

You may enjoy a compliment or an ego boost. Someone may repay a debt. This is a good day for a beauty or health boost. If you're working you may be asked for help or will need support yourself, which will be available to you. ***Moon enters Leo.***

## 14 September

This is a good day for making changes in your personal life or within shared arrangements, at work and financially; you may change some aspects of an agreement. A change of pace or of place will certainly feel empowering, even if events seem intense as well. ***Moon in Leo.***

## 15 September

You may be surprised by news from a group, friend or organisation. If a disagreement with a friend arises it may be due to a fundamental difference in values. A financial matter may be the source of developments. ***Moon enters Virgo.***

## 16 September

This is a good day to be practical about what you want. Consider how you can go about making the changes you want in life. Tomorrow's new moon will be the ideal time to make a wish, so work out what you'd ideally like. Romance could blossom but you must avoid misunderstandings. ***Moon in Virgo.***

## 17 September

The new moon supermoon in Virgo is ideal for setting intentions to boost your relationships and improving a commitment that can seem intense; this applies both to work and your personal life. A financial plan could be ideal so you can afford a special trip or break. ***Moon enters Libra.***

## 18 September

You may experience crossed lines, so be super clear about what you're trying to communicate, especially at home. Ensure you have all the right information, and if you realise you don't do your research. ***Moon in Libra.***

## 19 September

You are dynamic at the moment and have high hopes. You know how to attain your goals but may tend to pre-empt outcomes today, so be patient and avoid snap decisions. Work hard and your efforts will be rewarded. ***Moon enters Scorpio.***

## 20 September

The Scorpio moon may bring your idealistic side out, as the moon aligns with mystic Neptune, the planet of dreams. Be realistic. You'll enjoy a trip to the ocean or the chance to enjoy music and creativity. Spiritual crabs could gain deep insight. This is a good day for meditation and it could be a romantic evening.

## 21 September

As a water sign you are intuitive. Today, you may feel someone has power over you or is intense. To avoid arguments, channel your energy into creative matters at work or into making your home your castle and relaxing haven. ***Moon enters Sagittarius.***

## 22 September

As the sun enters the sign of Libra this is the equinox, when day is equal to night. This is a good time to check you're on course and that you're not compromising your values in the face of other people's pressure on or influence over you. Aim for balance and compassion moving forward. ***Moon in Sagittarius.***

## 23 September

The key to success lies in being patient, as this will help you avoid arguments or a sense of being restricted by someone's opinions or stubbornness, especially with authority figures. Have the facts if you're under pressure, and channel frustrations into good work. You'll enjoy a reunion or hearing from an old friend. ***Moon in Sagittarius.***

## 24 September

Words will flow. You may be inclined to be impulsive or act out of character. If someone you know behaves rashly, aim to restore balance to the situation if possible. Be reasonable and practical and you could make great headway. ***Moon enters Capricorn.***

## 25 September

The more practical you are the better, especially at work and with conversations that are challenging. There may be merit in going over old ground to ensure you are on the same page as someone with whom you must work or collaborate. ***Moon in Capricorn.***

## 26 September

Ensure your actions align with your values to avoid confusion or a sense of being disappointed. Finances may require a little focus. You may experience some tension with someone close. Romance could blossom despite stress. ***Moon enters Aquarius.***

## 27 September

You'll enjoy a get together with someone close, such as a family member, or someone you love or admire and look up to. Romance could blossom, but if negative feelings are expressed avoid taking them personally. A visit, get together or trip will be food for the soul. ***Moon in Aquarius.***

## 28 September

You could make great progress at work and financially, so take the initiative. An interest, venture or project could steam ahead. A lovely relationship will feel empowering. If an obstacle arises, consider an alternative idea; you'll get the chance to mull over your plans in the days to come. Trust your instincts. ***Moon enters Pisces.***

## 29 September

You may decide to review a work-related or personal commitment. Talks over the next two days may reveal a vulnerability, your own or that of someone close. Be careful with finances; avoid impulse buys and check receipts. Someone may ask for your help. If travelling, plan ahead to avoid delays. Keep communications clear to avoid mix-ups. ***Moon in Pisces.***

## 30 September

The lead up to an Aries full moon can be intense as it will spotlight a venture, project or interest you are invested in. Avoid snap decisions and aim to work off excess energy at the gym or the beach or simply through being actively involved in interests you love. ***Moon in Pisces.***

# OCTOBER

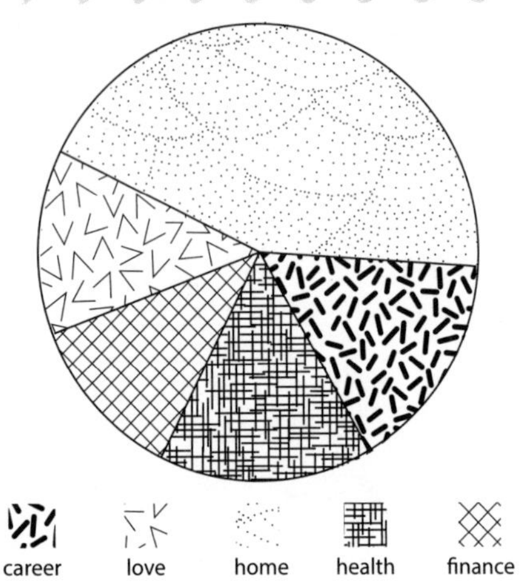


## 1 October

Tomorrow's Aries full moon will spotlight a work project, venture or interest. You may be asked for help or may need support yourself. For some, the full moon will spotlight a vulnerability; for others a strength. You may wish for a fresh agreement with someone or to be seen in a new light.

## 2 October

The full moon will amplify your ability to be adventurous, strong and outgoing. If logistics seem complex at first, you will overcome challenges. You'll enjoy doing something different this evening, and a get together or a relaxing evening at home will appeal. ***Moon enters Taurus.***

## 3 October

With the moon in Taurus for much of the weekend you'll enjoy the opportunity to find some relaxation doing the activities you love with people you love. You'll enjoy music, dance, socialising and family time.

## 4 October

An old argument or point of tension that you thought was over with or resolved may re-emerge. The moon in Taurus will motivate you share positive experiences with those you love and look for paths to move forward in practical, realistic and down-to-earth ways.

## 5 October

The Taurean moon will encourage you to take things step by step, especially your relationships and communications. If you feel that some interpersonal dynamics at work or at home are simply inescapable, consider how you could change these. ***Moon in Taurus.***

## 6 October

Repeating past mistakes can be frustrating, especially when you know better or you know someone else knows better. Avoid contributing to mistakes and find different ways ahead if possible. New opportunities may arise over the coming days, so be ready to make the most of your options. ***Moon enters Gemini.***

## 7 October

You may be surprised by unexpected developments. Someone close may behave unpredictably or you may be seen as being unpredictable. You may bump into an old friend. Be ready to adapt to something new or different. Take the time to discuss your ideas and thoughts with someone you know has a balanced outlook. ***Moon in Gemini.***

## 8 October

Someone you know from your past may be a significant influence. If current developments remind you of something from your past, avoid allowing this to affect your present. You could excel with a project but you must be well organised. Avoid conflict, as it could spiral rapidly. ***Moon enters Cancer.***

## 9 October

If you work well under pressure you'll enjoy today's developments and could excel, but you must avoid buckling under intense pressure. For some crabs, today's Mars–Pluto square will translate as tension or a potential disagreement that could spiral, so avoid escalating arguments. Look for ways to channel excess energy into upbeat pursuits. ***Moon in Cancer.***

## 10 October

You may be surprised by developments, and these could lead to improved self-esteem or even a financial boost. Events will gain their own momentum, so be happy with your direction or be prepared to apply the brakes when necessary. You may disagree with someone, but must find a calm way to overcome differences. ***Moon in Cancer.***

## 11 October

You are a strong character, but you can feel daunted when challenges arise. Luckily, the Leo moon will bring your sunny side out. The arts, music and spirituality will nurture your soul. Avoid arguments and look for solutions instead. ***Moon enters Leo.***

## 12 October

You'll feel inspired and this will be a great start to the week, as you'll enjoy infusing your days with an upbeat feeling. You'll enjoy a trip somewhere beautiful and touching base with a friend or partner. Romance could blossom, but you must avoid putting too much pressure on yourself and others. ***Moon in Leo.***

## 13 October

Combine your progressive approach to life with practicalities and you could move far ahead. An unexpected call or development may demand you think on your feet. If you have particular personal or domestic matters you wish to float, try to do so before Mercury begins its retrograde phase tomorrow to avoid delays and mix-ups. ***Moon enters Virgo.***

## 14 October

You may be surprised by the intensity of someone's opinions. Decisions can be made but you must avoid impulsiveness, or you may need to review your choices at a later date. A trip may mark a change in a significant relationship. Be ready to try something new and to float good ideas. ***Moon in Virgo.***

## 15 October

You could excel but you know better than to oppose someone when they are in a mood. You'll appreciate the chance to get down to the nitty gritty with several matters in your personal life and at work, but you must avoid power struggles. A disagreement with someone needn't turn into conflict. ***Moon enters Libra.***

## 16 October

Tomorrow's new moon supermoon in Libra represents a brand new phase in your personal life. This may translate as a fresh chapter domestically or in a close relationship. If you are a creative or musical crab you may begin a fresh project. Avoid locking horns with someone you must collaborate with; look for solutions instead.

## 17 October

The new moon together with Mercury in Scorpio can produce deep and powerful insight into yourself and others; conversations may be intense. Be careful with your interactions, especially with a business or personal partner. A domestic or family matter may require delicate handling. Romance could sizzle but you must avoid conflict, as it will spiral quickly. ***Moon enters Scorpio.***

## 18 October

Ensure you have all the details if you're making important statements or have key negotiations to undertake, especially if these involve finances or your long-term future regarding work, relationships or home. You may only have part of the picture. This is a good day for art, music, meditation and spiritual activities. ***Moon in Scorpio.***

## 19 October

This is a good day to make changes at home such as enriching the décor or improving the ambience. Relationships can blossom, so if you have bridges to mend this is your day – as long as you're willing to listen to someone's opinions and don't make snap decisions. Be super clear and reliable. Avoid overspending. ***Moon enters Sagittarius.***

## 20 October

An unexpected change of circumstance at home or at work or an impromptu event may put your routine out of sync, but you should enjoy a get together or a change of scenery. ***Moon in Sagittarius.***

## 21 October

The changes you wish to make at home, in your social life, your partnership or at work should progress. You'll enjoy a lovely trip or meeting that may have a transformational effect in your life. Romance can blossom, so singles: get set to mingle! ***Moon enters Capricorn.***

## 22 October

You'll enjoy a lovely get together, and a trip or an outing to somewhere dreamy will appeal. You'll be inspired by art, design, film and music. Artistic crabs will enjoy today's creative vibe. ***Moon in Capricorn.***

## 23 October

You'll enjoy being sociable and allowing your creativity to shine at work. You may enjoy a lovely trip somewhere beautiful and will appreciate the arts, music and dance. Romance could blossom. ***Moon enters Aquarius.***

## 24 October

If you're working it will be a particularly lucrative or productive day. It's an ideal day for a working bee at home and to make domestic improvements. You could make a wonderfully strong commitment to someone. The sun in Scorpio for the next four weeks will ramp up the passion in your life. ***Moon in Aquarius.***

## 25 October

Developments, a visit or news at home or to do with property or family will be important. You'll enjoy a trip, even if logistics are complex at first. Romance could blossom, so make space for relaxation. ***Moon enters Pisces.***

## 26 October

You may have a slight case of Monday-itis if you're working. If you have the day off you'll enjoy daydreaming and being creative and spending time with those you love. Research all the details, especially if you're making key decisions or commitments.

## 27 October

You should feel you're getting on a little better with someone you must collaborate with at home or at work. Take time out when you can to establish peace and calm. Avoid daydreaming at work. ***Moon in Pisces.***

## 28 October

A visit or a trip should be enjoyable. You may receive a guest or experience domestic improvements. You may also benefit from an ego boost, and some lucky crabs will enjoy a financial boost. ***Moon enters Aries.***

## 29 October

Today's Aries moon should feel motivational; you may even gain the chance to boost finances or your status. This will be a productive day but you or someone close such as a colleague may tend to be super sensitive. Take the initiative, but avoid rash mistakes.

## 30 October

You should find the evening settling after a busy day, but the lead-up to the full moon may feel intense. Take the time to discuss your plans with those they concern and opt to dispel tension.

## 31 October

Tomorrow's Taurean full moon will spotlight your interests, activities, relationships and social life, and you'll gain insight into how to progress in your favourite areas in practical terms. Be prepared for a surprise, which needn't be bad: this is Hallowe'en, after all!

# NOVEMBER

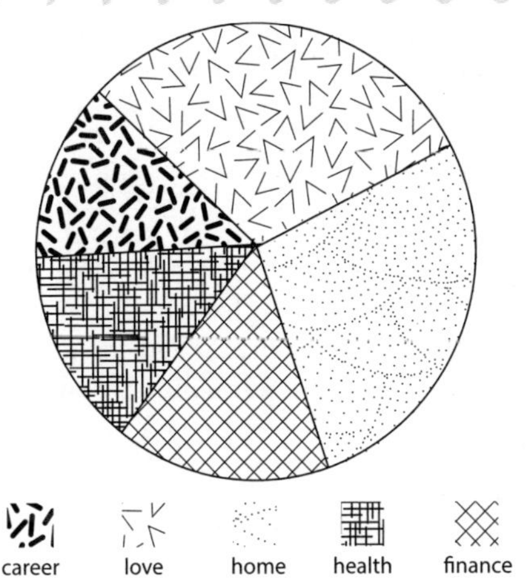


## 1 November

The full moon is shining intensely, and there may be disagreements or a challenge. These could concern domestic matters or health, shared ventures and money. Misunderstandings could be rife, so avoid mix-ups. Be ready to make agreements rather than arguing. Romance will blossom for some lucky crabs. ***Moon in Taurus.***

## 2 November

The moon at the zenith of your chart will feel revitalising, especially in your relationships. Take the time to get in touch with like-minded people and to seek agreements with those you love.

## 3 November

You may receive distinct news that will signal the end of an uncertain phase or a process that has left some communications and developments up in the air. Key agreements can be made, but you must be sure you are not limiting your options. ***Moon in Gemini.***

## 4 November

Stay on top of unexpected or tough developments, even if they seem to be counter-intuitive or are against your values. You should manage to overcome any obstacles. A change in your usual routine may involve a complex schedule or logistical difficulty. Try to stick with your plans but be adaptable to changes. ***Moon in Gemini.***

## 5 November

When the moon is in your sign you are super intuitive, so rely on your gut instincts. You'll enjoy being creative, and spiritual endeavours should flourish. Romance could blossom. ***Moon enters Cancer.***

## 6 November

You may need to go over old ground or reiterate some of your viewpoints, especially regarding home and work. Be flexible, but also be prepared to stick to your values. Be realistic and practical and avoid arguments for the best results. ***Moon in Cancer.***

## 7 November

As a water sign you do not like to be rushed. Today, you may need to take rapid action in a particular venture, which may feel frustrating. Once you take action, however, you should overcome any hurdles. ***Moon enters Leo.***

## 8 November

Today's Leo moon will feel motivational, especially in your personal life and creatively. Don't be afraid to take the lead. Romance could flourish. Sports, outdoor activities and work could all flourish as well.

## 9 November

You may need to work out your priorities so that you avoid having to choose between events and duties, and between what you want and what someone else wants. A lovely get together at home or a meeting at work will be inspiring or productive, but you must avoid locking horns. You'll enjoy art, music and romance. ***Moon enters Virgo.***

## 10 November

This is a super romantic day and could manifest as a chance to add candlelight to your home or to enjoy art, film and dance with someone you love. You'll enjoy a meeting or get together. Ensure you have all the right information at your fingertips to avoid mix-ups and delays. ***Moon in Virgo.***

## 11 November

There may be a head-in-the-clouds aspect to your day. You'll find out if you've been unrealistic about a project, domestic matter or relationship. If your expectations have been too high you'll get a reality hit, which will enable you to make amends and be more realistic in the circumstances. ***Moon enters Libra.***

## 12 November

A development could make a considerable impact on your life, so be clear about your options and about how you'd like to move forward, especially in a relationship, at work or regarding health. ***Moon in Libra.***

## 13 November

Friday the 13th! This needn't be a frightening or bad luck day, and in fact you can positively affect your closest business and personal relationships today. It's a creative day for music and art. Keep those you love in the loop, even if some talks seem intense at first. Romance could flourish. ***Moon enters Scorpio.***

## 14 November

This is a positive day for get togethers, be these romantic, with friends or family related. You'll enjoy changing your environment for the better, and this could include a little DIY at home. ***Moon in Scorpio.***

## 15 November

Today's Scorpio new moon supermoon marks a transformative time, most notably in your personal life and creativity. For some the new moon points to developments at home. It's a good time to transform the areas of your life you know need revitalisation. Events may gain their own momentum, so ensure you are happy with the direction in which you're heading or prepare to make changes.

## 16 November

You can accomplish a great deal, especially at home and with someone special, but you must avoid pushing your agenda or your efforts may backfire. Act confidently and you could excel. ***Moon in Sagittarius.***

## 17 November

Be prepared for a surprise, or you may surprise someone yourself. Developments may be out of the ordinary. A trip may take you somewhere unusual. Avoid misunderstandings and back up computers. Plan travel ahead of time to avoid delays. ***Moon enters Capricorn.***

## 18 November

You can't agree with everyone all the time, but you'll appreciate the sense that you can find common ground with a partner or someone you must collaborate with even if you have different mindsets. Be pragmatic and down to earth. ***Moon in Capricorn.***

## 19 November

You should begin to see the results of your hard work, be it in your personal life or at work. If you feel you've come to a Mexican stand-off with someone important, consider whether your mutual values are different and whether or not you can find common ground. ***Moon enters Aquarius.***

## 20 November

Take the time to discuss your various ideas and plans with those they concern regarding domestic, family and creative matters. You should come to a mutual understanding. ***Moon in Aquarius.***

## 21 November

You'll appreciate a sense of adventure that comes to you via a domestic or creative matter, and you should gain the sense that you can boost your status or circumstances as a result. Music, romance and dance will appeal. You'll enjoy being outgoing. ***Moon in Aquarius.***

## 22 November

You may dislike being pried out of your routine or your comfortable circumstances, so avoid ruffled feathers by being clear that you're in a dreamy state of mind and relaxation comes first! ***Moon enters Pisces.***

## 23 November

The inspiring Pisces moon will motivate you to focus on your favourite projects and people. You may be a little forgetful or absent-minded. The Sagittarian sun will add a touch of dynamism to your activities and at work that you'll enjoy. Trust your instincts and intuition.

## 24 November

The inspiring theme will continue, as you'll get the chance to show just how creative and romantic you are and how much you can achieve both domestically and with your various projects. Avoid being easily distracted or nothing will be done! ***Moon enters Aries.***

## 25 November

There is a therapeutic aspect to the next two days, so arrange a treat or aim to put therapeutic measures in place as the universe will support your efforts. This is a good time to ask for help with collaborations and to delegate work. Avoid snap decisions. ***Moon in Aries.***

## 26 November

This is a good day for a medical or beauty appointment. Meditation and spiritual practices may appeal. You may experience uplifting developments in your personal life or at home. Someone may offer to help. ***Moon in Aries.***

## 27 November

You may be surprised by developments; it will certainly be a good day to express yourself and to discuss developments at work and at home. A change of pace or environment may be unexpectedly refreshing. If you're working, developments may be surprising. You may receive an unexpected guest. ***Moon enters Taurus.***

## 28 November

Today's Taurean moon will help you to get your feet on the ground regarding recent developments in a partnership or at work. Take your time to decide how you will move forward in the most practical way. A get together with like-minded people should be enjoyable.

## 29 November

You'll appreciate the opportunity to get together with family and to take a trip somewhere beautiful that breathes fresh air into your lungs and revitalises your creativity and love life. ***Moon enters Gemini.***

## 30 November

Today's Gemini partial lunar eclipse signals a fresh chapter in your work life and status and, for some crabs, regarding your affiliation with a group, friend or organisation. Be ready to consider your circumstances from a fresh point of view and don't be afraid to gather information or do your research.

# DECEMBER

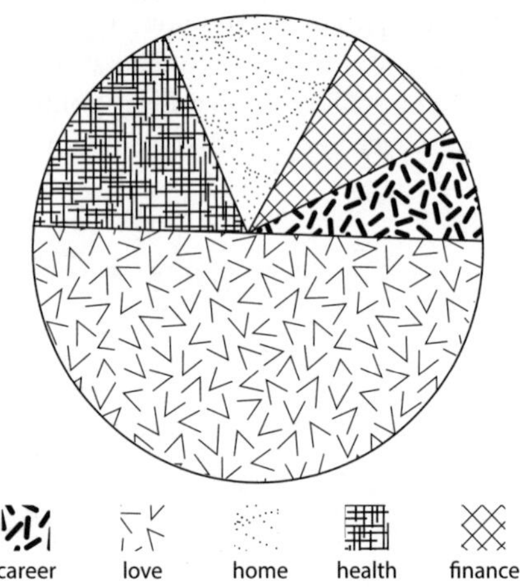


## 1 December

You'll enjoy hearing from someone from your past and getting ahead with your various projects. You'll also enjoy the chance to make some resolutions that you know can stick, especially with a business partner and in your personal life. Creativity should blossom. ***Moon in Gemini.***

## 2 December

Once the moon is in Cancer later today you'll feel more in sync with events and your intuition will be on full throttle, so trust your instincts if you have a key decision to make. Projects should blossom, especially when you employ your creative skills. ***Moon enters Cancer.***

## 3 December

You may wear your heart on your sleeve, so avoid reacting emotionally to someone's strong opinions. Tune in to your intuition, as this will help you to understand the undercurrents of events and maintain perspective. ***Moon in Cancer.***

## 4 December

You'll appreciate the opportunity to enjoy a favourite activity, art or musical event, but if you are relying on someone else to organise events you may need to step up, especially later in the day, and take some control of your plans. ***Moon enters Leo.***

## 5 December

You'll enjoy sport and outdoors activities; you may even surprise yourself with what you can achieve, not only workwise at home but also by engaging other people's interest in your activities. If you're working you may be busy. ***Moon in Leo.***

## 6 December

Plan ahead to ensure your activities run smoothly. An unexpected visitor or a change of schedule may need to be accommodated, but once you do you should enjoy relaxing. ***Moon enters Virgo.***

## 7 December

The moon in Virgo will boost your organisational abilities. You may need to pay bills, organise events or take an unexpected meeting. A lovely social get together will boost morale; start the week the way you mean to carry on! Take the time to address differences of opinion, especially with people with whom you must co-operate and collaborate. Aim for solutions.

## 8 December

Take your time to focus on details and be practical, especially regarding domestic matters and travel. Someone you admire will prove to be super helpful, so if you need a hand ask for it; support will be available both at work and at home. ***Moon in Virgo.***

## 9 December

When matters are up in the air it's important you bring them down to earth, but if this is impossible it's vital you're grounded and practical despite events being confused or even frustrating. Avoid being distracted. Avoid misunderstandings, mix-ups, confusion and unrealistic expectations. ***Moon enters Libra.***

## 10 December

This is a good day for romance, so plan something lovely. Singles may meet someone charming. This is also a good day to make agreements with people with whom you must collaborate. A person in a position of power may be particularly supportive. ***Moon in Libra.***

## 11 December

This is a good day for work and your favourite activities, so take the initiative and show your dynamic side. Avoid appearing feisty or pushing for results, as this will backfire. You should feel you're on the right track with your various projects. ***Moon enters Scorpio.***

## 12 December

Today's moon in Scorpio will strengthen your intuition. It's a good day for meditation, yoga and introspective pursuits. You'll gain deeper insight into someone you love and into a creative project. It's a good time to discuss important matters.

## 13 December

You may be super motivated to get ahead, but not everyone will feel the same. Someone with their head in the clouds may not be as enthusiastic as you. Consider your options, and if you need someone's support offer full details of your ideas. Avoid mix-ups and forgetfulness, overindulgence and impulsiveness. ***Moon enters Sagittarius.***

## 14 December

Tomorrow's total solar eclipse will spotlight a new chapter that will promise adventure and excitement – if you let it! For some, developments will be at work; for others they will concern health, home and family. This is a dynamic new moon that will encourage you to try something new. Obtain all the facts before making decisions. ***Moon in Sagittarius.***

## 15 December

During the eclipse phase great change is possible. You may be ready to make a new arrangement or agreement that could catapult you into a fresh relationship or understanding with someone, either in your personal life or at work. Avoid rash moves. Romance could flourish. ***Moon in Sagittarius.***

## 16 December

This is a good day for talks and discussions and for making agreements, especially in your love life, at work and financially. You may feel outgoing, optimistic and productive, so check details if you're making key commitments. ***Moon in Capricorn.***

## 17 December

As Saturn and the moon enter Aquarius prepare to think outside the square, especially in relation to your business and personal partnerships and in areas you share such as your duties or space at home. You may be asked to leave your comfort zone, but you will succeed.

## 18 December

This weekend you'll enjoy a change of pace or place. If you're working you're likely to be busy. You should gain a sense that you're on the right track, especially with a favourite venture, health-wise and with someone you love. Plan a healing treat or a meeting with someone you know always lifts your mood. ***Moon in Aquarius.***

## 19 December

An event may feel therapeutic or will have a healing effect on you. Be ready to embrace fresh dynamics in a relationship. You'll enjoy a trip somewhere new or to revitalise certain relationships by focusing on common ground, goals and interests. ***Moon enters Pisces.***

## 20 December

A change of pace in your usual Sunday arrangements may be delightful, but if plans are sketchy and to avoid arguments take steps to make things clearer. Be practical with arrangements for the best results. You may be ready to commit to someone. ***Moon in Pisces.***

## 21 December

The solstice is a time of reflection where you can gather your wits as you assimilate your progress so far. News may introduce something different at work, regarding health or in your daily routine, so be practical and realistic and you'll enjoy the spirit of Christmas and seasonal get togethers. ***Moon enters Aries.***

## 22 December

Now that the sun is in Capricorn it should provide a settling feeling, and you're likely to feel more practical about your various chores, relationships and ideas. The moon in Aries may produce a restless feel to the day, so slow down when possible and avoid arguments.

## 23 December

Being a water sign, your first response is emotional even though you are also highly intuitive. When developments take a momentum of their own, as they may today, engage your logic and be assertive or else intense changes or power struggles over the next two days may bring out strong emotions. ***Moon in Aries.***

## 24 December

Merry Christmas! The Taurean moon will stimulate your lust for life and enjoyment of good company: you'll enjoy good food and wine but must avoid overindulgence. A change in your usual routine and the predisposition to speak without thinking first may cause issues, so plan ahead if you're travelling and avoid misunderstandings.

## 25 December

Merry Christmas! You'll enjoy a change of pace or place and good company. There may be a surprise call or visit. Focus on the positives and good communications skills and not the negatives.

Avoid stubbornness and obstinate people. You may enjoy an ego boost or the chance to show off a little. ***Moon in Taurus.***

## 26 December

If you overindulged yesterday you'll appreciate the opportunity to relax today. There is a therapeutic aspect to the day. A sensitive topic or developments may be distracting. Avoid arguments that rake over hot coals. Someone may need your help or will help you. If you must work, aim to rest when possible. ***Moon enters Gemini.***

## 27 December

A change of atmosphere will be revitalising, so organise something different if you haven't already. You'll enjoy the upbeat and light-hearted atmosphere that the moon in Gemini will bring, and travel may take you somewhere you'll enjoy.

## 28 December

A trip or a change of routine will certainly feel energising. You'll appreciate the chance to do something different, and may be pleasantly surprised by news and developments. You'll enjoy a reunion, the return to an old haunt and the chance to connect with someone of a similar mindset. ***Moon in Gemini.***

## 29 December

You'll feel more at home as the day progresses, as the moon in Cancer this evening will reconnect you with someone you love or bring fresh dynamics into a difficult relationship. The next two days will be an excellent time to work on your plans for next year and to formulate intentions for 2021. ***Moon enters Cancer.***

## 30 December

Today's Cancerian full moon will kick-start a fresh phase in your personal life, especially if you were born at the end of June or in early July. Key talks may involve the need to discuss expectations for the new year, both at work and with family. Some lucky crabs will enjoy a get together and the chance to have an inspiring, nurturing, fulfilling time.

## 31 December

Happy New Year! You may feel emotional, so take time out to gather yourself. You may enjoy doing something different this New Year's Eve. A healing, positive approach to the new year will serve you well, and someone will wish to celebrate in the same way. Avoid overindulgence, or misunderstandings may arise. ***Moon enters Leo late at night.***

# Further information

Find out your moon sign and ascendant sign at astrocast.com.au.For your in-depth personal astrology chart readings contact Patsy Bennett: patsybennettastrology@gmail.com.

Further astronomical data can be obtained from the following:

- Michelsen, Neil F. and Pottenger, Rique, *The American Ephemeris for the 21st Century 2000–2050 at Midnight*, ACS Publications, 1997.
- The computer program Solar Fire from Esoteric Technologies Pty Ltd.

All astrological sun sign books are available in this series: Aries, Taurus, Gemini, Cancer, Leo, Virgo, Libra, Scorpio, Sagittarius, Capricorn, Aquarius and Pisces. Available online at www.rockpoolpublishing.com.au or at all good book stores.